Home at Last

DeWitt Smith

Home at Last

Published by Wheatmark®
2030 East Speedway Boulevard, Suite 106
Tucson, Arizona 85719 USA
www.wheatmark.com

ISBN: 978-1-62787-453-3 (paperback)
ISBN: 978-1-62787-454-0 (ebook)
LCCN: 2016952238

Cover photo by DeWitt Smith
Cover design by Jane Shanahan

This book is dedicated to Cynde Cherre and Stephen Kirschner, the two gifted therapists who helped while I dug my way out of the deep dark hole I was in.

Contents

Acknowledgments

I DEEPLY THANK the following people who took the time to read my manuscript while it was a work in progress.

Fellow journalist Leslie-Jean Thornton who did the first copy editing; friends and professional colleagues Ruth Campbell and Sarah Lewis for their feedback and encouragement.

I also thank former *Time* magazine writer and book reviewer, Stefan Kanfer, whose supportive words kept me going for more than a decade despite a dozen rejections from literary agents; and former newspaper colleagues Rita Ross, Mindy Spar, and Steve Sinovic for their keen eyes and encouraging remarks.

A very special thanks goes to Fred Miller, who was there for me as I moved through my last drafts and was also there when my father died. His unflagging emotional, financial and spiritual support kept me afloat as I slogged my way to the end.

In addition, I am indebted to the Palm Springs Writers Guild, which introduced me to Wheatmark Publishing President Sam Henrie and Director of Marketing Grael Norton, both of whom believed in me and my project. I'm so very grateful for their willingness to publish my book.

Shavertown, Pennsylvania
March 2017

1 *December 1992*

EVERY CELL IN my body was screaming for me to go faster. But I could only move at a crawl through the blinding rain. The windshield wipers were on high speed, and I still couldn't see more than twenty feet in front of my car. As I rounded the curve going down Gully Road to the beach, it was difficult to concentrate when the only thing on my mind was the phone call I'd gotten ten minutes ago: "Barbara, you'd better get down here. The house is about to go."

The tension between my mental speed and physical speed left me feeling a little schizoid, but the poor visibility forced me to drive slowly. When I got to the bottom of the hill, I could make out the blur of parked trucks along the side of the road, which was normally bare this time of year. I eased my Subaru behind the last truck on the road to my house, and with the engine turned off, the howl of the wind and the noise of the pelting rain were deafening.

I pulled my Nikon out of the camera bag on the passenger seat, and wrapped it in the terrycloth hand towel I brought with me. After slipping the strap around my neck, I tucked the camera under my slicker before getting out. The wind was so strong I had to push all my weight against the car door to get it open and keep it from slamming against my legs. I hunched forward and headed into the rain, which hit my face with such force it burned my skin.

Walking toward our driveway, I passed the New England Telephone Co. truck, the Yates Gas truck, the Nantucket

Electric Co. truck, two police cruisers and finally the Nantucket fire chief's red four-wheel-drive vehicle.

I looked up and saw a lineman hooked to the top of a telephone pole; he was cutting the wires away from all the houses. I did a quick scan down the road and saw a second lineman doing the same thing on another pole. On the right, there were a couple of police barricades across our driveway; on my left, two cops were keeping the gathering crowd behind the barricades. When I got to the top of the driveway, I saw two men coming toward me, carrying the large propane gas tank away from our house, which I still couldn't see through the rain. Suddenly I heard a snapping noise and watched as a telephone line whipped around in the wind. I also saw that there were no more electric or telephone lines leading to our compound. By then, I reached the policeman standing at the barricade.

"I'm Barbara Smith, the owner, and I'm going in," I said, trying to be heard above the wind. He nodded without a word and let me pass around onto the shell driveway. The entry to our property was about eighty feet ahead, and when I got to the archway, the sight was horrifying.

The house was on a steep pitch, listing like a ship about to go under. The waves were so high they hit the oceanside section of the roof. The waves kept flowing around both sides of the house, and I saw the sand being washed away from the foundation as I walked toward the front door.

Mark Fredland was standing there, and without saying a word, I gave this old family friend the key to the front door. When he opened it, I saw beyond the foyer that the water was gushing into the living room.

"Oh, my God," was all I could say.

I heard the wood groan as another wave hit the house, and the spray hit Mark and me. He signaled to two men, whose faces I couldn't make out, and the three of them ran into the foyer, lifted the credenza and carried it out of the house. Some more people ran forward and helped carry it to the garage on the other side of the archway. Mark ran back into Sandpiper.

When the next wave hit, I saw a woman running toward me. It was Elizabeth Churchill.

"Barbara, Barbara. Get him out of there. Get him out," she screamed.

I dashed to the top step, cupped my hands and yelled, "Maaaarrrk. Get out. Get out."

Mark came running out of the house with photos and paintings pressed against his chest with both arms. I motioned him to follow me and turned around to go into the second house on the property, about thirty feet in back of Sandpiper. Even though I didn't have a key to the door, I knew the sliding glass doors were unlocked. I ran and slid open the closest one, and Mark and I took shelter inside. Neither of us spoke, and I helped him unload the things in his arms onto the couch in the living room of Scoop's Coop, my father's two-bedroom cottage. Then it hit me— everything inside Sandpiper was going to go.

I wiped my sand-caked glasses. Stepping inside gave me momentary relief from the stinging wet sand and time to collect myself. As I looked through the sliding glass doors, I saw Rob Benchley on the deck between the two houses shooting with a videocamera. Rob was a colleague on the Nantucket Beacon, one of the island's two weekly newspapers. Seeing him reminded me that I was there on assignment, so I pulled my Nikon from underneath my slicker, stood at the open door and started shooting. That's when I felt myself start to fragment.

The left side of my brain knew I was shooting page one photos for next week's edition of the paper, and the right side felt overwhelmed by the emotion of seeing my home about to go out to sea. The left side saw that it was too late and too dangerous to retrieve anything from Sandpiper. The right side was going numb with disbelief. The left side was getting everything in focus through the lens; the right side was defocusing, as if everything were in slow motion, and the sounds of the people and the howl of the wind kept fading in and out like a far-away sound track. The left side knew I only had two rolls of film, so I was shooting judiciously. The right side felt I was in some strange movie that would soon be over.

The schizoid feeling was too much. I put the camera down and stepped back into the living room. Mark had gone out and returned, and, without a word, I went over to him. He put his arms around my shoulders. I put my head against his chest and could feel the tears starting. But I heard someone else come through the door. It was Mark's brother, Pete, and behind him was Rob with his videocam. He closed the sliding glass door and pulled out a towel from beneath his slicker to wipe the lens. Being inside allowed us to speak.

"This is unbelievable," said Pete in his low steady voice. "Two hundred-year storms in thirteen months."

"She's going any minute now, Rob," I said, and we both put our cameras up to our eyes as a huge wave came up, wrapped itself around the house and carried her off the foundation.

I got a couple of shots, put my camera down and stepped back outside and watched, stupefied, to see my three-bedroom house slide into the water and stay afloat like a ship. The house was actually riding the waves and, for a split second, I had the feeling I was watching the house in "The Wizard of Oz." Only instead of being carried off in the sky, the house was turning slowly, ever so slowly on the ocean. I saw her float with the current, and shot the last few frames of film as I watched the waves wash over the thirty-foot high brick chimney. Sandpiper was in a vortex, and as she slowly swung 'round and 'round, I saw a wave crash and break down the back wall of what had been my sister Betsy's bedroom. It was surreal to see the window boxes attached to the still standing outside wall, to see the lace curtains blowing through the two other window frames and see the white headboards of the twin beds.

"Oh, no, Mugsy's ashes. They're in Betsy's room," I cried out.

Mugsy was Betsy's yellow Labrador retriever, who had died three years ago, and Betsy had kept his ashes on her bureau in an urn wrapped with his pink bandanna.

The flood of memories stabbed at my heart.

Then another wave went over the top of the house, and another wall fell. With it, a spray of shingles flew away with the centrifugal force of the water and the wind. Even with this ferocious pounding, the house was still standing upright, a testament to how well houses were built seventy years ago. I brought the camera up to my eye and started shooting with my two-hundred-millimeter zoom lens, and stepped to the edge of what was left of the deck. Through the viewer I saw another wave go over the top and a geyser shoot through the house.

"The floor's gone," Mark cried out.

I tucked the lens back into the towel and slid the camera under my slicker. By now, I couldn't keep my eyes off the house and watched another wave crash over the three remaining walls. With that they fell outward into the churning ocean, and all that was left was a mass of wood, turning on top of the water like toothpicks.

I checked my watch. It was twelve-thirty, just a half-hour since I'd arrived. The sliding glass door to Scoop's Coop was still open, and I walked over and stepped inside to take shelter again. Mark, Pete, Rob and Elizabeth and David Churchill came inside, too, and we stood shoulder to shoulder, facing the empty space where Sandpiper used to be. Mark put his arm around me.

"Well, the poker game's on the way to Portugal," I said, referring to the years of late-night card games that took place in Sandpiper.

The five Smith sisters were all single, and over the years, we'd had a colorful collection of dogs and men. Sandpiper had been a magnet for free spirits on the easternmost shore of Nantucket, where we'd spent our summers since childhood.

Pete broke the silence.

"Let's get this stuff out of here into the garage. Scoop's Coop isn't going to make it either," he said.

I shuddered when I heard Pete size up the fate of Scoop's Coop, but knew it was true. That's when I snapped to. Dad's Jeep was in the garage, which meant there wasn't any room to store anything.

"Pete, I'm going to move the Jeep so there's room for the stuff from the house," I said as I started toward the open door.

"Okay, Barbara. Listen, Mark and I will take care of this. Don't worry," he said in a full-charge voice. I trusted the Fredlands and knew I wouldn't have to worry.

As I started toward the garage, my stomach knotted when I realized I didn't have the keys to the Jeep. My father's wife had refused to leave the keys with me when I asked for them in case of an emergency.

When I opened the garage door, I saw that the Jeep hood was up, and when I went around to the front of it, I saw why.

"Oh, the goddamn battery's been removed," I said out loud. I looked around and saw the battery sitting on a side counter.

Then I remembered Mr. Mauldin. Richard Mauldin was our caretaker, and his house was across Codfish Park Road, just on the other side of our driveway. I bet he had a set of keys. I ran out of the garage and turned right to go to his house. That's when I spotted Mr. Mauldin standing in his driveway watching the drama. The cop at the top of the driveway saw me come running and let me pass again. I ran over to the elderly man.

"Mr. Mauldin, do you have the keys to the Jeep and can you put the battery back in?" I asked. I explained about putting the furniture in the garage.

I could feel my voice start to choke up. "The boys are just moving the stuff now," I said.

This was no time to be politically correct. "The boys" I referred to were all men in their forties. On the other hand, Mr. Mauldin was ninety, so we were all "young people" to him.

"I've got the keys, and I'll be right over," he said.

I marveled at how fast and gracefully he moved. The elderly black man was probably a lot healthier than most of the 50-year-old white men on island and, without a doubt, more of a gentleman than many of the newcomers with their crisp, new money.

When I crossed the road to go to the garage, I saw two police officers standing at the front door of Mary Stackhouse's home. It was on the corner of our driveway and the road, and I could hear them try to convince her to evacuate.

"Mary, you've got to leave," said one of them urgently.

"No, I don't, and don't dare turn off my water. I'm staying," she said.

Mary was a tough old bird who worked as a nurse at

Nantucket Cottage Hospital on the eleven p.m. to seven a.m. shift. I looked over and saw that she was in her bathrobe. By now it was one p.m., her bedtime.

"Barbara," she cried out and waved. "I'm so sorry, dear. Who ever thought this could happen? Can I do anything for you? Do you and the dogs need a place to stay?"

"Thanks, Mary. I'm up at the Torrey house on King Street, so we're safe. I gotta go. We're getting the stuff out of Dad's cottage," I yelled.

As I passed the cop by the barricade again, I explained that Mr. Mauldin was coming with the key to the Jeep and to let him pass. He nodded again, without saying anything. Then I went running back down the driveway to the arbor. Seeing the empty space was a shock.

"If only I'd gotten there earlier to get some things out," I berated myself, and I felt overcome with remorse about not paying closer attention to the weather report. I also remembered how Mark had waited for me to arrive at Sandpiper with the key. It probably never occurred to him to break a windowpane to open the door without waiting for me. That's what I loved about Nantucket. It is a place where people still respected privacy and property.

By now, the encroaching waves had washed away the three brick steps leading to where Sandpiper's front door used to be, and the wooden benches that lined the deck were all gone. Those wonderful benches stood about eighteen inches off the ground and were six feet long. At night, we'd go outside to star gaze and lie down on the benches so we wouldn't get cricks in our necks. It was heavenly in August during the annual meteor showers.

In the morning my sisters and I sat on the benches while we ate breakfast and tossed tennis balls for the dogs over the dune that rose from the beach and stopped at our covered porch on the ocean side. My father used to yell his regular morning litany as he came outside to survey the day: "Get the damn dogs out of the dune grass."

"Yes, Dad," and my sisters and I would laugh at the futility of his plea.

Three of the Smith sisters had dogs, and the current canine count was three. Keeping the dogs off the dune grass was as impossible as keeping sand out of the house. The dune grass was the first place they went for their morning pee.

"Barbara, what's happening?"

The question brought me back, and I turned to see Mark and Pete standing in the open doorway of Scoop's Coop.

"Mr. Mauldin's putting the battery in the Jeep, and I'll have it out of there in five minutes," I said.

They nodded, and none of us said anything. The Fredland brothers were not only friends, but they'd done the remodeling work on Sandpiper six years ago and left their own mark of craftsmanship on the place. They knew every inch of the house. That's why Mark knew exactly where to go for the paintings and photographs he'd rescued.

"Don't worry about here. We'll take care of it, Barbara," Mark said.

I went over to him to give a quick hug and left.

The nor'easter was in full gale, blowing stronger than when I'd arrived. By this time, our next-door neighbor's house was gone, washed out to sea. I looked down the beach and saw Dr. King's house at a precarious angle. The wind and rain kept gaining momentum, and it took all my energy to walk forty feet to the garage. When I got there, Mr. Mauldin was closing the Jeep hood. As he gave me the keys, I said, "Thank you so much. I hope you and Mrs. Mauldin will be all right. I'm up at Torreys if you need to call."

He nodded and said, "Thanks. We're back far enough to be safe."

I got into the car, put the key in the ignition and the Jeep started up right away. I let the engine run for about five minutes to charge the battery and then backed out of the garage.

When I got to the top of the driveway, I rolled the window down and recognized the police officer coming toward the Jeep. It was Charlie Gibson, the assistant police chief.

"Hi, Charlie. It's Barbara Smith. This is a helluva storm. I suppose you saw the house go out."

"Yeah, I did. I'm sorry, Barbara."

"Listen, don't worry about the moving the barriers to let me out," I said. "I'll drive around Bank Street to get up Gully Road. But I've got to come back to get my car after I park my father's Jeep upbank. My Subaru is parked behind the telephone trucks."

"Okay, Barbara. When you come back down, just make your way to me to get through. Drive carefully."

The power and telephone crews had done their work, and the men were standing along the edge of the driveway watching the next batch of houses go out.

By now, four policemen were busy moving the barricades back along the far side of the road to keep the growing crowd of spectators from getting in the way. I looked up at the top of the bluff and was startled to see people all along the wood railing. There was a stream of people with videocams and cameras coming down the cement stairway from the bluff to Codfish Park, despite the whipping winds and flying rain and sand.

"Thank God the heater in the Jeep works," I thought as I started to feel chilled to the bone. "Well, at least the numbing is wearing off and I'm feeling something."

With a flip of the psychic switch, I became the reporter instead of an ex-home owner and decided to take a quick look around Codfish Park to check out any other damage. I turned right at the top of the driveway to drive the half-mile loop that went around the park.

I spotted an ambulance at the Wilson's cottage and saw someone helping Mrs. Wilson into the back of it. Someone else was bringing out Mr. Wilson in a wheelchair. I realized the elderly couple, both in their nineties, were being evacuated. "Probably to the hospital," I thought.

I made a mental note to call their daughter. As I looked on my right, I could see her two-story house take a pounding. Twenty-foot waves were spraying off the side of the house, which was still holding strong. It was farther back from the water than ours had been. Seeing the next property gave me a jolt.

It was Chris Holland's old house, and the waves were breaking over the front section of the building. I'd always loved this little house with its widow's walk and picture windows. I remembered when Chris and his wife, Linda, bought the property and built the place. My fiancé and I used to have dinners with them, and afterward we'd sit out on their deck to watch the stars.

I drove around the bend, back along Bank Street. On the leeward side, out of the howl of the wind, it was much quieter. I finished the loop and reached Codfish Park Road again and headed up Gully Road.

By now, the heater had warmed my feet and hands. The gloves I had worn were soaking wet and useless, and I discarded them on the front seat. When I got to the rotary at the top of the hill, I did a quick logistical check. If I drove the Jeep back to the Torrey house, I'd have to walk half a mile in the storm to retrieve the Subaru. Better to stay here by the 'Sconset Market, just a block from the bluff.

I parked the Jeep and headed back down to Codfish Park, and swore at myself for not wearing my slicker rain hat. Even though the knitted tam hadn't protected my hair from getting soaked, at least it was keeping my hair out of my face. I made my way through the crowd, a wall of bright yellow slickers and matching storm hats, much like a huge field of daffodils. When I got to the bottom of the steps I saw Charlie Gibson, who let me through. By now I was feeling the first strain of fatigue, and I was hungry, angry, tired and cold.

I just wanted to get home. My rain boots felt heavy and my right shoulder ached from the weight of the camera and two lenses. I finally reached my car, struggled to pull the door open, got behind the wheel and got it going.

In the three-minute drive back to King Street, I remembered why I wasn't living down in Codfish Park now. Six weeks ago I'd had a premonition about a bad winter storm. After my father left in October for his winter home in Florida, I was supposed to move into Scoop's Coop, just like I had done last year. But a small, inner voice kept telling me not to move back into the cottage.

Two days before I was due to move, I called a cousin who had a summer house in 'Sconset and made a deal to rent her house for the winter. She was happy for the rent money; I was happy to feel safe. My sisters and father all made fun of me for paying rent when I could live rent free.

"Don't ask me why, but I'm afraid of a storm," I told them.

So I'd gathered my clothes and papers and computer and some of my favorite pieces of art from the Codfish Park houses and moved up to King Street. I'd also moved my boxes of linens, china, silverware and all my little things that I'd brought from Miami to feather my nest.

I parked the car and ran to the front door. As soon as

I opened it, my two dogs came charging out. Maggie and George hadn't been out for over twelve hours. They relieved themselves quickly and came back to the front door in a flash. I hung my slicker over the closet door, took off the hat and sat down to take off my boots. As cold as I was, I wanted to do a couple of things before I hit the shower. I turned on the tea maker and saw that the electricity wasn't out. "Good, that means hot water," I thought. I put an English muffin in the toaster and brought out the peanut butter for a quick hit of protein.

Before I went to the bedroom, which was directly off the big L-shaped kitchen, I walked over to the washing machine, striped off my wet clothes and put them in the machine. The chaos of the morning brought an overwhelming need for some order. I went to the bathroom, put on my robe and slippers, grabbed a towel and wrapped it around my head to dry my hair. Then I went to my bedroom, where I fell to my knees by the side of the bed in an exhausted slump.

All my emotions were catching up with me. As the sobs started, I was so grateful I'd listened to my instinct to move. Because I'd paid attention to that little voice, the dogs and I were not left out in the cold, scrambling for a place to stay, and I still had my few worldly possessions.

When the sobs stopped, and I could feel my body and mind start to calm down, I heard myself say out loud: "Thank you, God, for keeping me safe."

I got up off my knees and headed for the shower. It was time for some water therapy, to warm my cold skin and tired bones.

2 *The Background Years*

THE FIRST TIME I went to Nantucket was in 1949, when I was seven, to stay with my grandmother at her summer home. When I was sixteen, Granny died, and my father inherited Paddy-Go-Wack, the name of her house (all the houses on Nantucket have names). Granny's death in 1958 meant Peggy, my father's second wife, took over Paddy-Go-Wack. That's when Peggy exiled me from the island.

Three weeks after Peggy died in 1978, my father bought Sandpiper. It was very different from Paddy-Go-Wack, which he sold in 1969. Sandpiper was a beach house on a half-acre, and my father had his own winterized bachelor cottage, named Scoop's Coop, built behind the larger cottage. Dad had a large deck built to connect the two houses, and he turned Sandpiper over to his daughters, the "girls house" as he called it. We all came and went as we pleased, and Harrison (I always referred to him by his name) relished being the merry widower. He was never short of invitations from the many widows and divorcees in 'Sconset. He also had friends and cousins on island whom he'd known for a lifetime.

Harrison was ensconced in Scoop's Coop from Memorial Day to October, and at least three of the five Smith sisters visited or stayed in Sandpiper during the summer. In addition, there was Richard, Betsy's friend from Pennsylvania, who spent the summers with us. Richard took on the role of baby brother and court jester. The daily routine was for Richard to appear on deck mid-morning, or in the living room when it was foggy, while the sisters were in various stages of sleepwear and breakfast. More than likely we were also in various stages of being hung over. Richard was always very zippety-do-dah and dressed, and he'd appear with a pitcher of Bloody Marys.

The daughters held out their empty glasses while Richard poured the mother's milk of vodka and tomato juice.

During the day, there was tennis up at the Casino or swimming and sunning on the beach, just forty feet from our front porch, or walking up to the village to get the mail at the post office. Harrison had his own daily routines. One of his highly visible activities—he was never low visibility—was his mid-afternoon swim. He'd fix his usual cocktail—rum and grapefruit juice—in a large Styrofoam cup, walk up the beach about fifty yards and, with his plantation hat firmly on his head, wade into the ocean, until he was about ten feet offshore. Then he floated on his back, sipping his cocktail and raising his cup to people he knew on the beach, until the current delivered him in front of Sandpiper, at which point he turned his body and ride a wave into shore.

At night if he didn't go to a cocktail party, he hosted his own. This was announced by running up his cocktail flag on the flagpole in the front yard. The cocktail flag was a pink elephant holding a martini glass in its trunk. Our friends and neighbors found it amusing. My sisters and I cringed.

Sandpiper had its own gatherings. Betsy was famous for giving dinner parties and was equally famous for the mess she left in the kitchen, including burned pots and pans. She'd put something on the stove, go out on the deck for a cocktail and completely forget that she was cooking. Someone, usually not Betsy, would eventually wander into the kitchen to turn off whatever was burning. And it became a ritual to buy new pots and pans to replace all the burned ones at the end of the summer.

After dinner, there was music and a poker game, a friendly penny-nickel-and-dime game, with lots of drinking and smoking and laughing.

I snapped out of my reverie when the shower water had warmed my bones. I dressed and got ready to head into the office, and called my boss before leaving the house.

"Hi, Kurt. It's DeWitt. Have you heard about Codfish Park? Sandpiper's gone," I said. My voice tightened on the last sentence.

"Yes, I've heard. Rob's here, and I've seen the videotape. I'm so sorry, DeWitt. How are you doing?" he asked softly.

"I'm feeling a little fragile, but I've changed and had something to eat. So I'm coming in. I've got two rolls of film of the house going out. I'm going to need more film because the rest of the houses on the beach are standing targets, unless this storm blows out tonight."

"No, we're in the thick of it for three days. I've been monitoring the weather report, and the winds are doing sixty-five, and the sea surge is hitting the Cape as well as Nantucket," he said. "But don't feel that you have to come in."

"I really don't want to be here alone. I'd rather be at the office where I can do something. Looks like we've got the front page for next week. Are the computers up? Is there flooding in town?" I asked in a torrent. The mental switch had flipped to the left lobe, and DeWitt Smith, the reporter took over the conversation.

We talked for five minutes, and then I left, with the dogs curled up on my bed. I felt better once I got to the office. As the senior reporter—in age as well as experience—most of the time I came up with my own story ideas, turned in clean copy, had my own camera and shot a lot of photos. On closing night, I also edited stories and did some layout.

Four months after arriving on island, I started working at the Beacon for twenty hours a week. In addition to earning enough to cover my food and gas costs (my weekly salary of $150 netted me $135), the Beacon also gave me professional satisfaction and entree into the community. Most of all, it gave me a sense of family. The editorial staff consisted of four reporters, two photographers and the editor, and we all put our hearts and a lot of hustle into our work.

When I got to the office, I had a conference with Kurt about the front-page story on Codfish Park, including a first-person feature about losing a house.

Afterward, I went to the Stop & Shop market to get food and supplies. The store was open—a nor'easter was no reason to close—and busy. That's when I learned how fast news traveled on the tom-tom circuit. People came up to me, some of whom I knew and others I didn't, to express their sympathy and to ask if there was anything they could do. I was so touched that I started to cry. The sense of loss was beginning to seep in, but I swallowed hard to stop the tears.

On the drive back to 'Sconset, I couldn't stop the "if only I'd paid attention to the weather report" tape that was running in my head. Poor Rosanne and Betsy lost everything they owned—clothes, jewelry, papers, photographs, furnishings. Just two weeks earlier, I'd sent Rosanne her passport for her upcoming trip to India. Before she left the island in October, she'd packed her bags and left them in her room. The two suitcases had washed out with Sandpiper.

I thought of all the other things, big and small, that were gone: the linens, dishes, wonderful old wool blankets with satin edging, books, glasses, the appliances like the washer and dryer and stove and refrigerator. Again, I blinked the tears back. I didn't want to cry now. But today's loss re-activated the wound I'd gotten eighteen months ago when I lost all the contents of my house in Miami.

It was dark by the time I got back to 'Sconset. I let the dogs out and then called my father.

"Hi, Dad. It's Barbara. I've got bad news. We've lost Sandpiper."

There was a three-second silence before he responded.

"Tell me what happened," he said in an even voice.

I gave him the blow-by-blow description.

"There's been no letup with this storm, and the forecast says it's here for two more days. Mark and Pete and some of the guys emptied out Scoop's Coop. I moved the Jeep up here to the Torreys to make room in the garage for all the stuff in your cottage. The way it's blowing, it'll be a miracle if Scoop's Coop survives this storm. It was heartbreaking to see Sandpiper go," I said, and realized this was the first admission I'd made about the loss.

Usually by six o'clock, Harrison was in the midst of his cocktail hour and couldn't always be relied upon for sensible conversation. Tonight he was dead sober.

"We've been watching reports about the storm. Thank God you moved into the Torrey's with the dogs. Well, I just can't believe it."

"I know, Dad. I saw it happen, and I still can't believe it. I'm going to call the girls and let them know what's happened."

"Call me tomorrow, dear, to let me know how things are."

"Yes, I will, Dad," and I could feel the tears start to come again. This time I didn't try to hold them back.

I hung up and, as I sat on the edge of the bed, I thought, "God, I'd love a good stiff drink."

As a recovering alcoholic, I'd stopped drinking years ago, so there was no alcohol in the house. Even so, I still wanted to have a drink to take the edge off the creeping pain.

Instead, I made a pot of tea and called Betsy, who was in Maine. There wasn't any answer, so I left a message. I couldn't reach Rosanne, who was staying at an ashram in western Massachusetts.

After dinner, I watched the news on a Boston TV station for updates about the storm. The news clips showed the widespread damage on the Cape and Islands, and the report confirmed what Kurt had said—the storm system would be stationary for two more days.

I turned the set off and lifted little George, the twenty-five-pound beagle mix, onto the bed so he could take his place under the covers with me. Maggie, the ninety-pound black Labrador, was in her dog bed on the floor.

When I awoke, the first thing I heard was the pounding rain and the howling wind. The storm hadn't let up at all. I showered, ate a big breakfast and dressed warmly, this time tucking my corduroys into my rain boots and wearing my slicker hat. I headed back down to Codfish Park, but the top of Gully Road was blocked with barricades. So I drove around the rotary, parked in front of the 'Sconset Market and walked the same route as yesterday. There was another crowd gathering, as if watching houses washing out to sea was a spectator sport.

From the stairway I saw that the waves were the same thirty-foot walls of water as yesterday. When I got to the bottom, the police officer from yesterday let me pass to get to the property.

Today's sight from the top of the driveway was even more shocking. In twenty-four hours, the ocean had washed away all the decking and the land in front of Scoop's Coop, leaving no access to the front of the house. If Mark and Pete hadn't emptied the cottage yesterday, today would have been too late.

The only way I could get photos was to go to a neighbor's porch. From there I watched another neighbor's house fall into the raging surf and collapse. In minutes, the structure disappeared.

I turned around to face Scoop's Coop, the last target for the ocean. All the other houses were gone. The waves were crashing around the little cottage and sucking all the sand away from the still-standing flagpole. I smiled when I thought of my father's morning and evening ritual of running the American flag up and down the pole.

"God, if I'd only remembered to grab the cocktail flag yesterday, I could have run it up the flagpole one last time," I thought.

Instead, I just watched as the ground washed away and the twenty-foot pole went crashing into the surf and was carried under. Then the waves were at the front door and took Scoop's Coop.

It didn't go like Sandpiper, which had floated out to sea with a sense of dignity, before breaking apart. Once Scoop's Coop was off its foundation, it tipped forward and fell dead onto the beach, anchored by the brick chimney. In twenty minutes, the gray-shingled walls were washed away. As I watched the land disappear, I realized I'd just witnessed my inheritance go out to sea. There was nothing left.

I thought about all the times my father emerged from his cottage at sunset to stand on the edge of the deck and, with a drink in one hand, he gestured expansively with the other one and say to nobody in particular, "Look at Daddy's North Atlantic Ocean," in a great proprietary voice.

It became a family joke, and sometimes when my sisters and I were sitting on the deck, we'd look at each other and say in unison: "Look at Daddy's North Atlantic Ocean."

"Daddy ought to see his fucking North Atlantic Ocean now. It's washed everything away," I thought.

3 *December 1992–January 1993*

WHAT REMAINED WAS the family legacy of alcoholism.

My father is an alcoholic; his current wife doesn't go a day without a drink (he is her second alcoholic husband); his second wife (the stepmother who raised me) was an alcoholic (as was her mother and brother); two of my four sisters are alcoholics; my father's brother was an alcoholic; his sister was an alcoholic (she died at age 53); my paternal grandfather was an alcoholic; and I strongly suspect that my paternal great-grandfather was an alcoholic (two of his four daughters married alcoholic men); I married an alcoholic. I'm an alcoholic. I hate this goddam disease.

Alcoholism is a big cheat. It cheated me out of a normal childhood and family life. It cheated me out of a healthy marriage (I broke my engagement to a man who was not an alcoholic and ran off to marry an alcoholic.)

The legacy of the alcoholism has had a stranglehold on my four sisters and me. We seem to have an internal radar that propelled us into the arms of alcoholic men who combined the worst of both parents: emotionally absent and highly critical. If the men weren't alcoholic, then they were self-centered and narcissistic. Much like dear old dad, their idea of a conversation was a monologue.

Growing up in this emotional desert has left deep, invisible wounds on the five of us. No wonder that not one of the five daughters had any children. It seems as if we took a tacit vow never to pass on what had happened to us.

Now that the houses were gone, a new element for the Smith sisters emerged: not only we were husbandless and childless, we were homeless.

After being a widower for eleven years, my father remarried. Dorothy, who had never been to Nantucket before she met my father, convinced him to build a house for them away from the compound. The salt in the wound was that the wife of three years was going to have a house on Nantucket, and my sisters and I, who had been coming to Nantucket all our lives, were left with nothing.

The storm had delayed the mail for four days. Finally, on Wednesday, I went to the post office, like everybody else in 'Sconset, to pick up mail. Located on the rotary, the post office is the center of the village, physically and metaphysically. Anyone —resident or visitor—who needs some information simply asks the 'Sconset postmaster, Jim Ozias, the resident go-to guy.

Besides knowing everybody—who's on island, who's off island, where and how long—he also knows a lot that would make residents wince if they knew their secrets were not so secret.

While I was standing in line, the woman in front of me put some papers on the counter.

"Hi, Jim. Do you know who these people are? I found these photos on the beach this morning," she said.

Since I was taller than she, I was able to see over her shoulder without even trying. What I saw made me gasp.

"Those are my sisters and me" I cried out. "These were photographs that were in our house."

I moved alongside the woman and turned to her.

"I'm Barbara Smith, the owner of one of the houses that went out in Codfish Park," I blurted.

As I spoke, I felt the tears come.

"I'm so sorry about your homes, Barbara. I'm Edith Delker, and when I was walking my dog on the beach this morning, I had to watch where I was going because of all the debris the storm washed up. And I noticed these on the sand. Here, take them. I'm glad I found them for you."

The photos were of Betsy and Rosanne and Mugsy, and I asked if she could pinpoint where she found them. She said in front of the Summer House. Everybody who'd been chatting while waiting in line got very quiet. Jim stood there quietly until Edith and I left the post office. I wept as I walked back to the Torrey house and when I got inside, I went to the bedroom, lay across the bed and sobbed. George jumped up and was very still alongside me.

The phone rang, and I answered in a dull tone.

"Hello."

"Hi, Ba, it's Betsy."

"Oh, Betsy, finally. I'm so glad you called. Have you heard what happened?"

"Yes. Mark Fredland called. I can't believe it. I just can't," she said in a sad and shaky voice.

"I tried calling you in Maine, but all I got was an answering machine. Listen, the most amazing thing just happened," and I told her about the post office and the photographs. I had put them on the table in front of me as we were talking.

"I've been busy and haven't been able to get back to you," she said, her voice more composed now. "Frankly, I'm too depressed to talk about it. I'm going to a friend's for

Christmas and New Year's, and then I thought I'd swing down to Hyannis and catch the boat over to Nantucket for a day before I go back to Northampton," she said.

"I can't stand going down to Codfish Park by myself any more, Betsy. I get so depressed and then I get so goddam mad. Fucking Dorothy has a brand-new house and we don't have anything," I said. I could feel the rage in the back of my throat.

"I feel the same way," she said, and I could hear the anger in her voice, too.

"You want to stay here with me when you come?" I asked. "There's plenty of room."

"No, I'm going to stay at the Fredlands. Thanks, anyway. I'll be there the second of January."

"I'll hold the pictures until you get here. There's no point sending them to Maine," I told her.

"Okay, Ba. I'll see you. I certainly don't feel like it's a very merry Christmas this year," she said sadly.

"Yes, me, too," I answered.

I hung up and could felt a wave of depression come over me. The only thing to do was head to the office and get lost in work. I usually took the day off on Wednesday, the day the paper came out. But today I couldn't stand being in the house by myself.

At the office, I studied the paper. The photos were powerful, including the ones I took when I was in my disjointed state.

My phone rang, and my heart jumped when I heard the voice.

"Hi, darlin'. It's me. I'm coming up tomorrow for twenty-four hours, and I'll be on the one o'clock plane," said the warm, rich male voice.

"Oh, sweetheart. What a wonderful surprise," I said.

I'd seen Kent two weeks earlier when he was on Nantucket to close his house and drive his Jeep back to New York. I didn't think I'd see him again until mid-January. "How did you manage this?"

"I need to see you, baby, and I want to see you now, not in a month. I'm on my way to a meeting now, and I'm running late. And I won't have a chance to call tonight because of another meeting. I need you so much. Just twenty-one hours 'til we see each other. I love you, baby," he said.

Whenever Kent told me he loved me, I just melted.

"I love you, sweetheart. I can't wait," I said.

Kent lived just north of Manhattan and was married. The month before we met, in June, I'd made a list of all the things I wanted to have in a lover: a sense of humor, intelligence, curiosity, a love of music and literature, an interest in politics and psychology. I even put divorced on the list. The only thing I didn't put on the list was "not married."

Over the summer when he was on Nantucket by himself, we had long lunches and talked and laughed about so many mutual things we loved. It had been years since I'd enjoyed the company of an intellectual man. Spending time with him made me yearn for someone special in my life. He wore a wedding ring and made no secret about being married. In spite of that, we started our affair in September. I was so touch-starved, I had no will to resist. Three months later, it was still very new and hot.

He arrived, and we spent the next twenty-four hours in our own little cocoon. I'd never experienced sex with such freedom, and the passion made me feel so alive. When we were both spent, we fell asleep for a couple of hours.

When we got up, we showered and had some tea and fruit. While Moby Dick (my private name for him since he was a big fellow) was dressing, I built a fire with a gift he'd given me—a cord of wood, which on Nantucket was very pricey. We sat in front of the fire, in our dreamy state, and caught up with each other. Even though I spoke about the storm and the loss of everything, the swirling endorphins canceled out all the sad feelings. The only thing I felt was the afterglow of passion.

When the alarm went off the next morning, we were both too tired to do anything more than to kiss and hold each other. When I drove him to the airport, we said our goodbyes with great declarations of love. I watched the plane take off and stayed until I couldn't see it anymore.

Betsy arrived January second. I met her at the boat at Steamship Wharf and drove her to Mark's house. She was tired, and we just made small talk, avoiding the subject of Sandpiper.

"Just come by whenever you've finished having breakfast tomorrow morning. I'll be at Torreys," I said when I dropped her off.

"Okay, Ba," she said.

The next morning Betsy and I had a cup of tea before loading Maggie and George into the car to go down to Codfish Park. We got out of the car together, and the dogs followed us to where the entrance to the property used to be.

Betsy was shocked when she saw what wasn't there. The water pipes jutted from beneath the remaining sandbank, where the arbor used to stand. Everything else in front of that was now beach and water.

"Oh, Ba. I just can't believe it," and we jumped down onto the beach to the rear of where Scoop's Coop still lay dead on the sand.

It was low tide, which allowed us to walk along the side of the house. It was just a shell, its frame held together by the roof and chimney, which were partly buried in the sand.

The dogs ran down the beach, sniffing madly, and I wondered if they were confused about where the house and property went. God knows, I was.

Betsy and I walked along the beach so she could see what remained in Codfish Park. Three houses down from ours, a house was split open from the roof to the first floor, as if it had been cut by a giant paper cutter. The side facing the ocean was on display, just like a doll's house. It was bizarre to see the designer bedspreads still covering the twin beds and the matching curtains literally blowing in the breeze. Betsy and I didn't say anything. We just kept walking.

"Do you think we'll get enough insurance money to buy another place?" she asked.

"Who knows? Ours was insured by the feds, and their rate of reimbursement is much lower than a private insurer. The property assessment was $800,000. I checked at the assessor's office when I was checking the total loss of all the 'Sconset properties for the Beacon story. Even with the two houses, we'll be lucky to see $200,000. You can't even buy a parcel in 'Sconset for that," I said.

Betsy and I called the dogs, walked back to the car and drove up to the Summer House, a restaurant and guest cottages up on the 'Sconset bluff. We were silent as we walked back down to the beach where Edith Delker had found the photos from Sandpiper. We scoured the dune grass, which was littered with debris—pieces of wood from furnishings and interiors, and washed-up pink insulation that made the beach look as if it were strewn with cotton candy. But we didn't see anything of ours.

Back at the Torrey house, I gave her copies of the paper and the found photos. When she saw them, she started to cry.

"Yes, I know, Betsy. It seems to come in waves."

"It's the same for me. It comes in waves. I didn't tell you over the phone, but I don't even have the things from here that I took to Maine. Someone broke into my car in Boston and took everything, even my Christmas gifts," she said. "Now, I don't have anything."

She started crying harder, and my heart sank for her.

"Oh, no, Betsy. I'm so sorry, sweetheart. If there's anything here that fits, you can have it."

I gave her some tissues and put my hand around her shoulder to hug her.

She blew her nose and stopped crying.

"Hey, Betsy, let's go to the thrift shop. You can get cords for fifty cents and sweaters for a dollar. The place is open until two o'clock," I said. "I bought my whole winter wardrobe there last year for about thirteen dollars."

"Oh, what a good idea, Ba. I'm going into town anyway. If I can't find anything there, I'll go to Murray's," she said, referring to the clothes store.

We went to the thrift shop, where she got some winter things, and I took her back to the Fredlands.

"Bye, Ba. I'm getting the morning boat, so I won't see you for a while. I don't plan to be back until late spring, and I don't know where Rosanne and I are going to spend the summer. Frankly, I don't even want to think about it."

My own waves of depression were coming with greater frequency, and nothing seemed to ward them off, not even walking the dogs. I wasn't sleeping well, I lost my appetite, and a lethargy set in. The only thing that buoyed my spirits was the thought of celebrating my fifty-first birthday at the end of January with Kent. We had plans for a rendezvous in Boston.

Five days before my birthday, he called to cancel. He

said his son, who was a crack addict, had to be in court for a jail sentencing that day.

The news was a blow, and it brought back the childhood feelings of when my father and Peggy were always absent on my birthday. They went to an annual newspaper convention in Philadelphia, and my birthday gift was usually a souvenir bag of items they brought back.

Kent's canceling our plans for my birthday slammed home the fact that I was involved with a married man, an unavailable man. He'd given me a ray of hope when he said a month ago that our relationship was forcing him to evaluate whether he wanted to stay in his marriage.

That night, the only thing I could feel was a severe pain deep in my stomach, and I had a flashback, to when I was four, when my mother left.

"Your mother is gone, and she's not coming back," someone told me. I don't know who told me, but those were the exact words. As a little girl I often cried myself to sleep, and no one was there to comfort me or stroke my hair or hold me, the way my mother used to. I was so alone, with no one to love me.

"Oh, my god. This whole thing with Kent cancelling our plans is about abandonment," I realized.

So *this* was the feeling that was frozen in my gut, that the person I loved had left me. I realized that I'd made a habit of avoiding this feeling of abandonment by being in a bad relationship rather than have no relationship at all.

The next morning I awoke, startled from a lucid dream. I reached for my dream notebook to write it down. Even though I couldn't make any sense of it, the dream left the same deep impression that my inner voice did about moving out of Codfish Park. I knew I had to pay attention to it.

I made my cup of tea and retrieved the new Omega

Institute catalogue in the living room. Omega was a summer campus about an hour north of Manhattan, known for its workshops and programs for spiritual and psychological development. I leafed through the catalogue and saw that a dream workshop was scheduled to start today in Lakeville, Connecticut. Even though I couldn't afford it, I called the eight-hundred number, just for the hell of it, to see if there was any space left in the workshop. There was.

I showered, dressed, had breakfast, let the dogs out and then drove to the office. I sat at my desk and made a few calls for a story I was working on, but last night's dream wouldn't let me alone.

"I've got to get to that workshop," I heard myself say out loud.

I looked at my watch. It was noon, and I could feel my mind go into high gear. Inspired, I called a good friend in Miami and asked if he'd be willing to pay for the workshop by credit card. He said yes, and I gave him the 800 number. He called back in five minutes and said I was registered.

"Oh, Jerry, thanks for being such a good friend. Thanks for your generosity. I'll repay you when I get some money," I told him.

"Don't worry. I know you're good for it, my dear."

I called Nantucket Air to check the flight times to Hyannis. There was a one-fifteen flight available, and I made a reservation. With that, I went into the editor's office.

"Kurt, can you lend me some money until Wednesday, payday, so I can get away for the weekend?"

Without asking a question, he reached into his wallet, pulled out a credit card and gave it to me. "Enjoy," he said.

I ran to my desk to make two calls: one to reserve a rental car and another to a friend to have her dog sit for the weekend. When she said yes, it took me a half-hour to make the trip from the office to 'Sconset, pack a bag and get to the airport. I got there at ten after one.

The burst of energy felt good, and it lasted for the five-hour drive from Hyannis to the Lakeville Inn, just in time to have dinner before the first session at seven-thirty. When I sat down, I said, "I was driven to get here."

The man leading the group was Robert Bosnak, a Jungian dream therapist from Cambridge, Massachusetts, and without wasting any time on introductions, he started immediately. He asked if anyone wanted to explore a dream. A hand went up, and right away the group of fifteen got to experience how Bosnak worked. From all the questions, it was clear that everyone had been in therapy.

After the first session, the group stayed in the big room for tea and to chat. Before going to my room, I went for a walk in the fresh snowfall. Lakeville is one of those picturesque little towns in northwest Connecticut, and it felt good to see hills and towering pine trees.

"I wouldn't mind living here," heard myself say aloud.

I had thought Nantucket was going to be my forever home. But the storm had changed all that. Now I realized I was going to have to move off island.

In the morning session, I got to work my dream. The process was simple: the group sat in a circle while the dreamer told the dream. Then, one by one, people asked questions. The dreamer did not answer, just listened to the questions. The next step was a minute or two of silence so the group could absorb everything that had been asked. Then the dreamer retold the dream, giving as much detail as possible. If the dream involved a room, the dreamer described the room in detail. Finally, in the same order, the people re-asked the same question. But this time the dreamer answered.

Bosnak cautioned us against jumping to any easy interpretations about the meaning of a dream.

"It's important to listen to the feeling and then listen to the content. The second time the dreamer tells the dream, the feeling is to be submersed, like a submarine, to move out of the head, to listen here," he said, moving his hands from his temples to his heart.

As I reached for my dream notebook, Bosnak said quietly, "Don't use your notebook. Just try to tell it as you remember."

I put my notebook down and started.

"I'm driving in Italy. It's a warm spring day and I'm driving a red convertible with the top down. There's no traffic so I'm moving easily, and I'm wearing a cotton dress. I'm feeling free and easy. I'm headed for Florence to meet a friend in a café. I pull up to the café, get out and enter it and see Pedro at the bar. I notice that I'm the only woman in the bar, and I realize I'm in a gay bar. I order some tea, and Pedro and I are speaking Spanish. We're both very animated as we catch up with each other. The light starts to dim as the afternoon gets late. A salmon-colored light over the bar comes on, so that the two of us are bathed in a cone of soft light. I feel so free, so happy.

Suddenly, I look at my watch. It's nine o'clock. I jump off the bar stool and, in English, I say: 'I've got to get to Rome before midnight.' I run from the café, get in the car and drive off to Rome."

"That's the end of the dream," I say.

There room was silent, and then people started to ask their questions. When they finished, I retold the dream.

The room was quiet, and the first question was asked.

"How do you know you're in Italy?"

"The road signs are in Italian," I answer.

"Have you ever been to Europe?"

"Yes, I lived there for two years, in Paris, Madrid and London."

"Do you have any gay male friends?"

"Yes. I worked as a model and met lots of gay men. Then over the years I have made friends with other gay men."

"What's the feeling in the gay bar?"

"It feels very safe. I'm comfortable and no one will hit on me."

"What does Florence mean to you?"

"It means a city of art, of artists, of creativity. There's an air of beauty."

The room is silent for a minute or two.

There's a long silence.

"Do you know anyone by the name of Pedro?"

"No."

Another silence.

"What does Rome mean to you?

"All I can think is that all roads lead to Rome."

"Were you raised in the Catholic Church?" Bosnak asks.

"No."

More silence.

"Is it Rome, the city, or is it R-O-A-M?" Bosnak asks.

"It's the city."

Then someone asks a question that wasn't asked before.

"Have you ever been without a home?"

I'm stunned.

"Six weeks ago, my house..." and I start to sob. "My house was washed out to sea. And everything in it. The furniture, the clothes, all the paintings my grandmother did."

I sat weeping in my chair, and the person next to me gave me a box of tissues to wipe my face. And I continued.

"Now I know what Florence means. It's where my grandmother studied art. I associate Florence with my grandmother, who was the only source of love when I was little. And before I moved to Nantucket, my house was robbed. The thieves stole all my grandmother's silver and all my jewelry. The only thing left was a salmon-colored cameo that my grandmother got in Florence that she gave me when I was sixteen."

Through my tears, I felt weightless and far away.

"What does the Cinderella tale mean to you?" Bosnak asks.

"My parents were divorced when I was four. My father got custody of my two sisters and me, and he remarried six months later. My stepmother was terribly cruel and physically abused me. After my mother left, no one ever said I love you," I sobbed. "I was Cinderella."

I'd gone as far as I could with the dream.

Bosnak explained that we weren't gathered to resolve anything, that it was important to remember "life's a process. Frankly, I think closure is highly overrated."

4 *The Early Years*

MY EARLIEST MEMORY is from 1944, being on a sled, my mother pulling me in the snow while my father took photographs. That was at a winter home in Bear Creek, outside of Wilkes-Barre, Pennsylvania. The next memories are from Glen Summit, the summer home on the other side of the valley. I remember sitting on the grass with Laddie, my father's English setter, and watching my mother play tennis. Afterward, when we drove home, she let me stand on the running board on the driver's side, and I hung on as she made the short and slow drive home. I remember her laugh as I squealed with delight. I was three and a half years old.

Then everything changed. My father went away. I didn't

understand there was a war going on. While my father was in Asia, a nursemaid named Mamie worked for my mother and to take care of my younger sister and me. And I spent a lot of time with my grandmother.

Going to Granny's was always a treat. I helped her plant cherry tomatoes in her Victory garden, the home gardens Americans had during the war so the big farms could supply food for the troops. Carl, my grandmother's butler and chauffeur, would put the spade in the ground, and I'd jump on the top edge to push the metal into the dirt while holding onto the long wooden handle. When I jumped off, Carl dug the spade into the earth, to make a hole for the next tomato plant. And we'd start all over again. I also remember helping Granny put the tomato plants into the ground and wrap the stalks with string to attach them to wooden stakes.

There was also dancing and singing. My mother had a collection of records—I still recall the black and gold Decca label—mostly big-band music and a lot of Frank Sinatra. Mother taught me the words and how to snap my fingers in time to the music, and I'd dance around the living room by myself while the music played. By age four I'd started my life-long love affair with singing and dancing.

Then, everything shifted again. My father came home, my mother left and Mamie stayed. Someone, I don't know who, told me, "Your mother is going away. You won't see her any more."

Shortly after that, my father remarried, and he, his new wife and Marjorie and I moved into a new house, away from where my grandmother lived.

The memory of my stepmother's first conversation with me is chilling.

"You can call me Aunt Peggy. Just don't call me Mommy because I'm not your mother. Your mother abandoned you.

Mother animals kill their children before they let anyone take them away from them. Only a horrible woman would abandon her children."

Her words and growling tone of voice left me mute and confused. That was the message she repeated throughout my childhood—"Your mother abandoned you"—with such regularity that it was like acid etching the words into my psyche.

Shortly after that, Peggy fired Mamie. In a period of six months, my dog was gone, my mother was gone, and my nursemaid was gone. And there was no more music and dancing.

In addition, I no longer had my own bedroom. My old room had three bay windows and was airy and light. Marjorie and I now shared a bedroom, which was dark. Even in the morning, I had to turn the light on in order to see. There was a bunk bed, and Peggy assigned me to the top bunk, which was very difficult getting up and down and into without bumping my head on the ceiling. I remember two things about living in that house. The first spring, when I was six years old, I was sitting on the lawn with Peggy and my baby sister, Susan. She had just come to live with us (my mother had been awarded custody of her until she was twenty-two months), and I was delighted to have a new baby sister. Susan, a beautiful little girl, had been crawling on the lawn. She crawled over to Peggy who ignored her. Then, in a bid for attention, Susan bit Peggy's arm. Peggy yelled angrily, "I'll show you," grabbed Susan's little arm and bit it so hard I could see the teeth marks left on the baby's skin.

Susan screamed with pain, and Peggy snarled in what became a lifelong nasty tone, "That'll teach you."

She got up, grabbed Susan by her baby arm and yanked her across the grass with her feet dragging behind her, much like a doll. I was left sitting on the lawn, wide-eyed and terrified.

At nighttime, I remember lying in bed with my teddy bear, and not being able to feel my body. I would try to wiggle my toes to see if they were still there. And then I would try to wiggle my fingers, but I couldn't feel anything. I also remember sometimes being so angry, I would suddenly sit up, grab my teddy bear, punch it and then throw it as hard as I could down on the floor. Horrified at what I had done, I crawled out of the top bunk in the dark to fetch my little brown bear, pick it up in my arms, stroke it softly and cry, telling it, "I'm sorry, I'm sorry, I'm sorry."

We were in that house only seven months before moving to another house farther out in the country. My little brown bear got lost in the move. After that, I never had another toy or a doll. Now everything was gone.

The name of the place we moved to was Shrine View, a cul-de-sac with eight other big houses.

Shortly after the move to Shrine View, Peggy and my father had their first child, Rosanne. And the following year, Betsy was born. And so Shrine View became the family home.

Built on terraced slopes, the big white clapboard house had four floors. On the bottom was a game room that ran the length of the house. The first floor had a kitchen, a bedroom, a dining room, a living room, and a den with French doors leading to a flagstone terrace overlooking a rock garden. The third floor had six bedrooms and three bathrooms. The top floor was the attic, the place for any unused furniture, cedar chests and cedar closets to store the off-season clothes. There were several bookcases for books and stacks of old National Geographic magazines.

At the end of the attic was a small room where my father's war things were stored. In the center was a big, old leather trunk that contained lots of children's kimonos that he had brought back from Korea, where he had been stationed, and two swords that my grandfather had during the Spanish-American War in the Philippines and in Cuba. Stashed away in the trunk were photos and papers and love letters Pop Smith had written to my grandmother.

"My dearest girl," the letters always began and were always signed, "Your loving man." In between, he described the scene from wherever he was, in France during World War I, in the Philippines or Cuba during the Spanish-American War. In Cuba, the Colonel, as my grandfather was known, had commandeered a buckboard and saved the lives and belongings of a rich Cuban family. In return, the grandee gave my grandfather a large cut and polished emerald, which Pop Smith had set in platinum and diamonds and gave to my grandmother as an engagement ring. This is what my grandmother told me. And I loved seeing the large emerald and diamond ring on her finger.

Reading my grandfather's letters created a lifelong love of romantic and adventurous stories. No wonder the attic was my favorite place. It was also an escape from Peggy.

When I was about seven, I remember rifling through all the papers in the bureau in the gunroom. I was looking for adoption papers since I was convinced that this was not my real family, and I desperately wanted to find my real parents so I could move. But instead of adoption papers, I found my baby book with my birth certificate.

Every chance I got, I slipped away to the attic to be close to the only evidence of love I could find, my pink baby book. I lingered over the inscription in my mother's handwriting: "This belongs to my sweet little daughter, Barbara, born to me on January 20, 1942. May her first seven years be as wonderful as her first day: bright and cheerful. And here's to her future with me. May we be real pals. Mother."

Each time I read it, I would clutch it to my chest with both hands and rock back and forth and cry. I learned to cry without making any noise, so I wouldn't give myself away. I was terrified Peggy would find the book and get rid of it, like everything else I loved.

When I finished going through my baby book, I carefully put it back in the drawer and would go through the other papers. I found some of the letters my mother had written to my father while she was in Reno, Nevada, getting a divorce. Back in 1947, Reno was the mecca for uncontested divorces. First, it only required a six-week residency, and second, all other states granted divorces on two grounds only: adultery or insanity.

My mother's letters told how much she missed her three girls and that she hoped Peggy was being kind and loving. Even at that tender age I knew kind and loving were two traits Peggy did not possess, not to the day she died. What she loved was being Mrs. Harrison Harvey Smith, wife of the newspaper publisher. She loved the social status and privilege that came with the marriage. The two other things she loved were talking on the telephone and alcohol.

It was also clear what she did not like: children and getting out of bed in the morning. From the start, my sisters and I were left in the care of nursemaids who lived with us. But the turnover was frequent.

We started with the French nursemaid, Georgette; then Phyllis, an English nursemaid who kept throwing her empty beer cans in the furnace, which caused it to go out. And when the furnace went out, my father would go down to the furnace room where I could hear him swear: "Jesus Christ. Who put the goddam beer can in the worm? The goddam furnace is out."

Next was a couple, Olive and Lloyd. They didn't last very long and were fired when they tried to leave Nantucket with our car after a fight with Peggy. After they left, there was Nana, a sweet Jamaican woman who came to live with us just as I was entering sixth grade. By then, I was ten and suicidal.

I used to wonder what it would be like to jump off a bridge into the river, or run out in front of a car. One time I climbed a tree and jumped from the top, only to break my arm.

At any mention of my mother, Peggy would fly into a fury. It could last for hours or for days, depending on how much she had been drinking. Every time my mother called, Peggy would stay on the line, and when the conversation ended, I'd have to endure her dripping sarcasm and mimicking everything my mother had said. And when my mother's letters arrived, Peggy would make me open the letters in front of her and read them out loud. Then she would start her mimicking all over again. I could feel the rage well up in me, but I was afraid of her. Being hit with her hairbrush or belt hurt, and besides, I learned that there wasn't anybody to defend me against this crazy woman. But I was determined to win this battle against her.

When I came home from school, I never knew how she was going to be. If Peggy was drinking sherry with a friend, then I felt safe. She was occupied, then she was too busy to pick on me. By the time her friend left, she'd be tipsy and she'd go to her bedroom to sleep it off before my father got home from the office.

Cocktails and cocktail parties were part of the norm around Shrine View, so much so that the first game my sisters and I made up was called "Janes and Marys."

After school, Susan and Marjorie and I would go down to the game room, get cocktail glasses off the shelves behind the long oak bar, and we'd fill them with Coca-Cola and maraschino cherries. Then the three of us sat around the big round coffee table and pretended we were drinking and smoking. Waving our candy cigarettes in the air, we'd puff and then blow away the imaginary smoke and call each other Jane and Mary, the names of Peggy's favorite drinking friends. It wasn't dolls for the young Smith sisters. It was martini glasses and candy cigarettes, and having our own cocktail parties, three little alcoholics in training.

Learning to deal with the big alcoholics in the household was a survival course. Staying out of Peggy's unpredictable mood swings required being on full-time alert, and it also required knowing how to move around with a great deal of stealth. From very young ages, my sisters and I learned to go up and down the front and back stairs without making a sound.

When there was household help, there was a lull in the insanity. But there was one incident that stuck in my memory. Georgette the French nursemaid had been fired, and Curtis the houseboy had left abruptly. Not too long after, one Saturday morning when I was up in my bedroom, I heard Curtis's voice in the kitchen. I immediately ran into my closet and hid. And when I heard Peggy call me, I sat crouched on the floor and didn't answer. Then I heard her say, "I don't know where she is."

I didn't come out of the closet until I heard his car leave the driveway.

The in-between-help stage was hell. In the morning, Peggy was usually hung over and wouldn't get out of bed, so no one fixed breakfast for my sisters and me before we went to school. I used to stand on my toes and reach for a couple of slices of bread in the breadbox and run out the door to the school bus. The bus picked us up early, before my father got downstairs.

No one bothered to dress us properly for school. I remember wearing cotton dresses in the dead of winter. No wonder I felt cold all the time. Even worse, often there were no clean clothes. I had to go to the hamper to get dirty underwear and dirty socks because my underwear drawer was empty. But worst of all was when I had to awaken Peggy to have her button my dress.

The first thing when I approached her was the awful smell. I had to shake her shoulder to awaken her and whisper and ask her to button my dress and fix my hair. Although I'd buttoned Marjorie's dress and fixed her hair, she was too young to return the favor.

The hair routine became unbearable. Once awake, she'd swing her legs over the side of the bed and button my dress first. She parted my hair in the middle and I handed her the rubber bands and hairbrush. Then she'd grab a handful of hair with such force it pulled my scalp. It hurt and I cried out, "Mumsie, it hurts." Mumsie was the name she insisted I call her after she got tired being called Aunt Peggy.

She'd hit my head with the hairbrush and snarl, "Be quiet."

My mother used to put a ribbon in my hair, and always made me feel pretty when she gently combed my bangs. There wasn't anything gentle about Peggy, and my scalp hurt for hours from where she'd hit me. Even before the bus got to school, I tore off the rubber bands to get some relief from the pain of my hair being pulled so tight.

With only two slices of bread for breakfast, my little stomach was in knots from hunger pains. I was chronically thin. One day at the start of the school year, the school nurse stated her concern because I was ten pounds underweight. A chart with the appropriate weight range for a given height was posted right in front of the scale, so I got to see the number for myself.

When the school sent a note home, Peggy took me

to see our pediatrician, and he also concluded that I was underweight.

"Perhaps a little sherry before supper would increase her appetite," Dr. Klein suggested after determining that I wasn't a picky eater.

So began the sherry therapy. That suggestion suited Peggy just fine, and she extended her afternoon dosage by a couple of more glasses. At the time, Phyllis the English-woman was the nanny in residence. The first night of my medicinal routine, Phyllis and Peggy had been drinking sherry together in the kitchen. I could tell by her tone and the way she spoke that Peggy was drunk. Although I'd never heard the word "drunk," I definitely connected the way she was behaving with the amount she'd been drinking. She was tipsy, and I could see the effort she was making not to slur or stagger. I could tell right away whether she'd been drinking. Her voice gave her away.

"Barbara, you sit here," Peggy ordered.

Right away, I was suspicious as I sat in the kitchen chair. Phyllis approached me with a small glass filled with a light yellow liquid. She put it to my lips and told me to drink it. It smelled awful, and when my tongue touched the liquid, it burned my mouth. I made a face and sprayed the little bit out of my mouth and cried out, "It burns my tongue."

In a flash, Phyllis held my nose, which forced me to open my mouth to breath, and Peggy poured the sherry in my mouth and then held my jaw shut so that I was forced to swallow. The burning sensation as well as a wave of nausea from the alcohol sent me into tears and I cried out, "My mouth burns. My mouth is burning."

I begged for a glass of water, and Phyllis and Peggy refused. They made me sit there, in tears, until they'd finished their glasses. Then they gave me a glass of water. This continued until the third day when I threw up all over the kitchen floor. Peggy fled from the room, and Phyllis had to clean it up. That stopped the sherry regimen.

By the time I reached sixth grade, I was still very thin. But now, I also had headaches and was exhausted by noon. Before lunch period, I would go to a teacher, ask for an aspirin, and lie down in a little rest room off the library. I fell into a deep sleep for probably an hour until the assistant principal, Miss Atwood, woke me up in time for to have a late lunch.

Once Miss Atwood asked, "Is anything wrong, Barbara?"

I started to cry but shook my head no. She had no idea that school was the only place I felt safe to sleep.

When Peggy came home drunk at night after dinner parties, I could hear her lurching around. And I was hyper vigilant until everything was quiet. One time she came staggering into my room (I always pretended to be asleep) and headed straight for my closet, where she took the box of all my photographs and letters from my mother and threw them out.

That same year I read "The Diary of Anne Frank." I loved the book and immediately identified with Anne Frank. I knew what it was like to live in terror and to have to hide to be safe.

There were two regular events that brought me some relief. The first was when Peggy would pick a fight with my father, which usually happened after a night of drinking. She would run upstairs, storm into Rosanne's and Betsy's bedrooms, drag them out of bed, putting coats over their pajamas, pack her suitcase and then run away from home for a couple of days. She went to a hotel in a nearby town.

"Oh, dear God, please make her die," I'd pray.

In her absence, my father and Marjorie and Susan and I enjoyed a peaceful house and tension-free meals. And as soon as she returned, the war zone resumed. We all started walking on eggshells again.

The second respite was when I visited my grandmother in Wilkes-Barre. I went there after school on most Fridays, and she had Carl, her chauffeur, drive me to dancing class. On Saturdays, Granny took me out to lunch and a movie. When we got back to her house, we usually went upstairs to her art studio to paint. Granny had Carl cut an easel down to size for me, and before she got busy working on her oil paintings, she set me up with watercolors or pastels.

And there we sat, the two of us at our own easels. I loved and treasured this time with her. And at night, when she tucked me in bed in the little girls room—the name she gave the guest room where Marjorie and I spent the night—she gave me a back massage and taught me to say a prayer: "Now I lay me down to sleep, I pray the Lord my soul to keep, If I should die before I wake, I pray the Lord my soul to take."

And she held me when she kissed me goodnight. It was even better when I went to Nantucket to stay at Granny's house. Far from Peggy's constant tirades, Nantucket was a place where I had playmates and fun and felt loved.

I always dreaded returning to Shrine View, and as Peggy got older, she got meaner and more unpredictable.

One evening I was sitting on the front stairs, watching Betsy do something in the kitchen. She was about two at the time, and for some reason Betsy started to cry. Peggy yelled, "Stop your crying." When Betsy didn't, Peggy picked her up by her ankles, held her upside down and started shaking her like a plunger. I watched in terror but was afraid to help. My body turned ice cold, frozen with fear. With every shake, Peggy's voice got shriller and shriller, "Stop it. Stop it. Stop it."

Poor little Betsy screamed in terror, and I remember thinking, "Peggy's crazy."

The daily criticism became a way of life, and I learned to protect myself with a poker face, to keep my seething and sadness inside.

Once, when I was having a defeated moment, Peggy spotted me and yelled, "You ungrateful child. What's the matter with you? You've got the best that money can buy. Get that expression off your face. How dare you."

This taught me that the only safe face to wear was one with a smile on it. She also constantly criticized my looks.

"The way you look, nobody but a truck driver would marry you," she said repeatedly.

My father was absent during these drunken episodes of hers. He was at the office during the day and often had community meetings in the evening, such as the Red Cross or hospital board meetings. When he was around, Peggy was on good behavior. All the verbal and physical abuse took place when he was gone.

She also threatened me into silence. "Don't you dare bother your father when he comes home from work. He doesn't have time to listen to you."

So the seed was planted: Look good, no matter what. That was the underpinning of the family myth—we were one big happy family.

Codes and secrets were part of the Smith family dynamic. One code was when my father and Peggy would speak French at the dinner table so the children wouldn't know what they were saying. That stopped once I started French classes at school. A large secret that was unknown to my father but known by Marjorie and me was that Peggy spent all day in bed, usually nursing a hangover. She didn't get up until we got back from school. That's when she ordered me to fetch her glasses of ginger ale or iced water to take to her smelly bedside (the odor of gin, worn-off Arpege, her favorite perfume, and stale cigarettes always made me gag). As I approached the bed, she'd say, as if to convince herself as well as me, "Well, you know, I do suffer from low blood pressure."

I was never convinced, and especially after I asked Dr. Klein, the pediatrician, about low blood pressure.

"There's no such thing," he replied.

Aha! A victory. I discovered Peggy's lie. That's when I also discovered the importance of gathering information and asking questions. I began reading the encyclopedia in the school library or at home to arm myself with knowledge.

Another thing Peggy never did was go to the market. She'd phone in an order from her bedroom and have it delivered. Since she never left her bedroom during the day, she didn't know what supplies were low or what was in the refrigerator. She simply asked the store owner what she needed and relied on him to keep track of past orders. At about four-thirty, she got out of bed, took a quick bath, dressed and went down to the kitchen to prepare dinner. By the time my father got back from the office, he was not aware that Peggy had only been out of bed for about an hour.

When I was in seventh grade, Nana, the Jamaican woman, left. After that, there was no more live-in help. That meant mealtimes were unpredictable. Because of the extended cocktail hour, dinner wouldn't be served until seven o'clock. Since I hadn't had anything to eat since noon at school, my hunger pains were severe. But if I went to the kitchen to get a piece of bread, she'd yell from the living room, "Get out of that kitchen. You'll spoil your appetite." I became a food thief to stave off hunger pains.

My father's abuse was different, and it took two forms. The first was benign neglect; the second was sexist. His routine at the dinner table was to ask a question, knowing that my sisters and I didn't know the answer. Then he'd say condescendingly, "You girls are nothing but a bunch of dumb goons. You had a fifty-fifty chance at birth and blew it. Now you're pathologically deformed." This was a nightly monologue.

Despite the stinging sarcasm and constant put-downs, I tried so hard to get his attention. I was an A-student and a good athlete, and everybody except Peggy thought I was well-behaved.

After dinner, when Peggy retreated upstairs to the phone, cocktail glass in hand. I went into the living room to be near my father, who was usually reading.

The living room had floor-to-ceiling built-in book-cases filled with beautiful leather-bound books that had belonged to my grandfather and great-grandfather. There were volumes of Churchill and Shakespeare and complete sets of Kipling and Poe. My father sat in his armchair by the fireplace with a book in his lap.

I remember when he was reading the six volumes of Edward Gibbon's "The History of the Decline and Fall of the Roman Empire" because, one night when I was there, he held up one of the volumes and announced, "What a pity. You girls are too dumb to understand this. Oh, well, you just can't help yourselves."

Feeling defeated, I left the room. I was only eleven years old, but the scar from those remarks left me with a lifetime habit of trying to prove myself. I tried harder and harder to show how smart I was, that I was lovable. If I tried hard enough, maybe someone would love me. That's all I ever wanted: to be loved.

Then, in the spring of 1954, my father snapped. One night I could hear him ranting and babbling in their bedroom, and I heard Peggy repeating herself, "What's wrong, Hal? What are you talking about?" And her voice became shriller each time she asked the same question. She fled downstairs to the phone in the front hall and called my father's brother, DeWitt.

Her tone of voice and frantic movement put me on hyper alert, and I stood very still at the top of the stairs to overhear the phone conversation. Eavesdropping was the only way I ever knew what was going on. Little did I know that I was training in the art of reconnaissance. That night's recon let me know there was an emergency.

"DeWitt, he's not making any sense. Please, you've got to get over here right away," she pleaded.

This was a new tone. I had never heard her sound scared. Keeping out of sight in the bedroom at the top of the stairs, I heard my uncle arrive and come upstairs. Once DeWitt was there, Peggy left the bedroom and went downstairs. I heard her make a drink before she made another telephone call. This time it was to my grandmother, and she became a little more composed. Even so, I could hear the strain in her voice.

When the conversation ended, Peggy went back upstairs and said to DeWitt, "Carl's coming."

Meanwhile, I could hear was my father's voice, talking incessantly. When Carl arrived, he and DeWitt helped my babbling father down the stairs and into Granny's car.

I learned the next day that my father was having a nervous breakdown, and Carl and DeWitt had taken him to the psychiatric unit of the University of Pennsylvania Hospital in Philadelphia. Within a week, Peggy rented an apartment in Philadelphia and took Betsy and Rosanne with her for three months. Marjorie, Susan and I were left at Shrine View with a housekeeper.

"Oh, God, peace at last," I thought.

A sense of order settled over the house. Ida the housekeeper made breakfast, saw that Marjorie, Susan and I were dressed properly for school, and supper was served on time and regularly. I spent weekends at Granny's, where occasionally I overheard her say to a friend, "Well, he's getting shock treatments, you know," referring to my father.

When he returned to Shrine View three months later, Peggy's focus was entirely on my father. She stopped hitting me, and the following year I went to boarding school, never again to live in Shrine View full time. I'd gotten out of that house alive, four years earlier than I expected.

5 *1956–1985*

GOING TO BOARDING school saved my life. I was out of Peggy's reach and in the care of people who ran an orderly, functional place. It was a small Moravian school for girls, two hours south of Wilkes-Barre.

Linden Hall is where I blossomed and thrived. In addition to having regular meals and clean laundry, it was safe to sleep. I had no distractions from my studies, which I loved.

I made the Dean's List the first semester, and joined the

Glee Club, the Drama Club, was on the hockey and tennis teams, and in my junior year took up riding. I was able to socialize freely because everything happened on campus. Linden Hall was also where I learned about reporting and writing. By my junior year, I was editor of the school paper.

I also started using my middle name as a first name. It solved the problem of what to call myself with four other girls named Barbara in my class.

At Linden Hall, there was no criticism, only encouragement and loving care. During my three years there, I grew emotionally and physically—four inches and thirty pounds. My stomach was no longer in nervous knots, and I was a healthy one hundred and fifteen pounds at five feet five.

Linden Hall was also where I got my first kiss, from a boy I met at a school dance. It was thrilling! And so were the ensuing love letters. He went to a nearby boys boarding school, and I went there for a spring weekend, when he told me "I love you."

At last, someone loved me. But Larry disappeared over the summer after our graduations. We went to our different ways, and he became a sweet memory.

The next stop was Syracuse University. It was a jolt going from a small girls boarding school, where there were twenty-five girls in my class to a freshman class of twenty-five hundred students. Many of the students came from New York City, and their reference points were very different. They were city girls, and I was fascinated to see how they got up at 6 o'clock in the morning for an eight-o'clock class because it took them an hour to do their makeup and hair.

I was housed in a cottage with ten other freshmen girls, eight of whom were also from small towns. I loved my new freedom. I could come and go as I pleased and only needed to observe the 10 p.m. curfew during the week and midnight on weekends.

Despite the good aspects, like learning how to date, I felt lost because of the size of the school. Basically, I felt disconnected.

This is where I also got drunk for the first time. Oh, god, it was awful. A date took me out for my birthday and bought us a bottle of Champagne. At the end of the evening, when I got back to my room and lay down, the room started spinning. I got up to put a cold washcloth over my face until I fell asleep. The next morning was my first hangover—I felt weak, dehydrated, fuzzy and cotton-mouthed. All I did that day was drink cokes and sleep.

But the hangover didn't stop me from drinking again. After that, I was more careful about my intake and made sure I had something to eat before I drank.

After too many parties and skipping too many 8 a.m. classes, I was on academic probation. Summer school would have put my grades right, but Peggy had her excuse to exile me. I remember her saying to my father: "Either she goes or I go." I was sent to live with my mother and her husband and their three children in Buffalo, New York.

Being shipped off meant I was removed from everything I knew, and I found myself living with strangers. I didn't know mother's husband or my two half-brothers and half-sister, and I hated sharing a bedroom with a 12-year-old girl. I really didn't even know my mother.

But luck was with me. The next-door neighbors hired me for occasional babysitting and liked that I was responsible. The husband was the manager of a nearby country club, and a month later, he hired me as a receptionist. The club was five minutes away from Mother's house.

The country club was my first job, and it was on-the-job training. I learned administrative skills and doing tasks at the reception desk. Most of the time I was dealing with club members and their requests, which gave me my first taste of public relations, which was fun for me.

Most of all, I liked earning my own money—two hundred and fifty dollars a month. That gave me enough money to buy a mini Morris, a little red convertible, the precursor of the mini Cooper. Little by little, I got to know my mother, after all those years of seeing her only once a year, on Christmas Day. Her husband, Ross, was a traveling salesman who was gone during the week. That meant Mother and I had time together, after the three younger children went to bed.

I loved getting to know her. We sat at the dining table and played gin rummy and talked and laughed. She was easygoing and had a good sense of humor. And she told me a little bit about her marriage to my father and how kind Granny had been to her.

After a year in Buffalo, my father called to say that he'd enrolled me at a secretarial school in New York City. Glory hallelujah! I was out of Buffalo. I lived at the Barbizon Hotel for women on the upper East Side and had my own room. My meals were served in the hotel dining room, along with the other Katherine Gibbs students. Best of all, I was able to make friends with girls my own age.

I loved being in Manhattan. I particularly loved walking down Park Avenue to school in the morning in my urban uniform (hats, gloves and suits were required). Because of the school's sterling reputation, Gibbs graduates were in high demand through its job placement office. Executives had bragging rights by saying, "My secretary's a Gibbs girl."

A week after I graduated, I was hired at an ad agency, at seventy-five dollars a week. That was a big deal in 1962, and I was able to afford sharing apartment with a Gibbs classmate. We found one on the upper East Side, near her parents.

Now I really was free! Living in New York gave me the chance to get rid of the ugly duckling label Peggy had pinned on me. I got contact lenses, had my hair done weekly and bought clothes that I liked. In addition to my salary, in 1963 I came into a small trust inheritance from my aunt, which gave me extra money for vacations and clothes. And at the ad agency, I was introduced to more sophisticated ways: humor, style and people.

New York was also where I first fell in love. He was funny, smart and came from "an attractive" (meaning a socially acceptable) family. Even better, his family liked me, and I loved feeling included.

But when I discovered I was pregnant, he said, "Well, I'll marry you and as soon as you have the baby, we'll get a divorce."

I was shocked at what he said. But that's when I discovered my strong practical gene. I saw the folly of being pregnant and unmarried. I also saw the folly of being a young, divorced woman with a baby. So I started researching about where I could get an abortion, which was illegal in 1963. I asked all the women I knew if they knew anything and followed every lead I got. There was a doctor in Ponce, Puerto Rico; one in Ashland, Pennsylvania; and I was referred to several shady men in New York City whom I didn't think were doctors. I shuddered leaving their dark, dank offices. Finally, I found an abortion clinic run by doctors in a New Jersey high rise. That ended the pregnancy.

But I got an aftershock when my sister told me she was sleeping with my boyfriend, the father-to-be. I was stupefied. It was too much for me to take in—a double hit and double betrayal.

"I wanted to show you what a shit he is," Susan said.

Shortly after the abortion, I decided it was time for a drastic change. I became a blonde, quit my job and ran away to Paris with money from my savings account and trust fund. But it was not gay Paree. It was January and cold, gray Paree, the perfect place for heartbreak hotel.

Even though I was staying with a friend from Syracuse University, I was lonely. I tried finding work at the U.S. Embassy, but there were no openings. My friend introduced me to some American women who wanted to drive to Madrid, and they were looking for a fourth passenger. On a whim, I joined them.

I was glad to leave Paris, be on the road and have some female company. The drive from Paris to Madrid took ten days because we stopped and toured almost every cathedral and old town. I turned out to be a big asset because I was the only one who spoke French.

As soon as we got to Madrid and checked into a hotel, I went to the American Express office the next day to have my mail forwarded from Paris. I also checked the American Express bulletin board and saw a notice that an American woman was looking for a roommate. I phoned her, we met and she seemed friendly enough. By the end of the week, I moved in.

My traveling companions understood when I said I was staying in Madrid. I had their itinerary if I wanted to catch up.

Francine, my new housemate, was a model. The same afternoon I moved in, Francine's agent called asking if she knew of an available model for a job in Majorca the next day. Francine suggested me. So I grabbed some headshots that were taken in Paris and went to the agent's office. She liked my photos, saw that I was photogenic, and the next morning, I flew to Majorca with the modeling crew and two ad agency guys for a weeklong shoot for a Thomas Cook travel brochure.

Hello, modeling career! Goodbye, heartbreak hotel.

Being a blonde in Spain meant I got a lot of work modeling for American products on Spanish television: "Usa Palmolive (Pahl-mahl-lee-vay.) Es fantastico." Same with catalogues for the American market. I flew all over Spain for modeling trips, including to Ibiza, Barcelona and Marbella.

I went to bullfights and dated Argentine polo players, was an extra in several American movies being made in Madrid, went skiing in Kitzbuhel, Austria, with Leka, the exiled king of Albania (who made his own visas and passports with his own royal stamps since he was the government in exile). I'm not making this up.

I met Leka when I moved to a new apartment behind the Prado Museum because he was a friend of my new roommate. Leka was very high profile at six-feet-10 and in his white Corvette, which he used to drive up to the Hilton, go into the bar to get banana daquiries to go.

Before we left for Austria, Leka introduced me to his mother, Queen Geraldine. She urged me to go with him over the Christmas holidays so he would have some lively company. She also asked me to call her Tante Gerry. So Leka and I went, with two Canadian friends of his also living in Madrid. Leka didn't ski and stayed at the hotel to read while I skied with the Canadians.

After a year and a half, I knew it was time to go back home, back to New York. But first I went to London to visit an old Linden Hall schoolmate. Two months later, I sailed to New York on the Queen Mary. I couldn't bear to fly back in seven hours; I wanted a slower re-entry after a year and a half of living in Europe.

I found a job and a place to live right away. The job was at Sports Illustrated, and the apartment was in Greenwich Village with the sister of my Madrid roommate. Barbara had just moved to New York from Madrid.

It was all so deliciously tra-la-la. I worked in the Time-Life Building, full of Waspy and preppy people. The building was filled with creative, curious, imaginative and good-looking men and women. It was like working at a country club.

Nine months later I was married at the Plaza Hotel, not to one of the Wasps, but to a man whom Peggy referred to as "the Russian Jew." Thanks to the Russian Jew, I had a very large solitaire diamond and a full-length mink coat, both of which Peggy drooled over. My mother-in-law made sure their family was not going to be embarrassed by the new bride in a cloth coat.

But the marriage didn't last very long, just eighteen months. Although Burt could be very sweet, he turned out to be highly critical and had a nasty temper. He fancied himself a movie critic, and when there wasn't a movie to criticize, he criticized me, which eventually wore me down. One night as I was folding the laundry, he started yelling at me for not folding his socks right. "Let him fold his own goddamn socks," I thought. The next day I moved out and was in a lawyer's office at noon. No more hissy fits, sarcasm, or scolding, just like Peggy.

I loved being single again. By this time, I'd moved from Sports Illustrated to Time magazine, the mother ship of Time Inc., where I worked for the managing editor and gained a whole new level of experience. Working at Time was like discovering a family I never had. Because of long hours over the weekend, when the magazine closed, the editorial staff members worked and socialized together. There was also plenty of pillow talk.

Because I was organized and good at public relations, I was loaned to the staff of the Public Affairs Department for a couple of months to work on one of Time's famous News Tours, given every four years. That year it was Southeast Asia, the news hot spot because of the Vietnam War.

Being on the advance team meant traveling ahead of the tour to prepare meetings and social events between the fifty captains of industry and heads of Asian states and U.S. ambassadors. We went from Manila, the Philippines—where President Marcos hosted the group for dinner on his yacht—to Saigon, then the capital of South Viet Nam; Singapore; Bangkok, Thailand; Kuala Lumpur, Malaysia; Jakarta, Indonesia; Seoul, South Korea; and Kyoto and Tokyo, Japan. We traveled in a chartered Pan Am 727 outfitted for first class, and limousines met the passengers on the tarmac. All of the CEOs had been issued U.S. Army camouflage uniforms for the South Viet Nam leg of the trip, and most of them had taken their uniforms to Brooks Brothers to be tailored. In addition to the exotic itinerary, the trip showed me I was nimble about fixing problems on the spot. As a result, I was considered a reliable team player. The experience gave me a new level of confidence about my career.

When I returned from the trip, I went back to the Time magazine staff for another year, at which time I was remarried. Peter Rient was a lawyer, and we moved to Washington, D.C., a year later.

This marriage started to unravel the night Peter and I went to a dinner party in the upscale neighborhood of Georgetown. While we were waiting for the host to answer the door, Peter looked at me and said, "You just stand there and look beautiful, baby, but let me do the talking."

Something inside of me snapped, and I knew I'd taken the blonde act too far. The next day, I had my hair cut and colored back to red auburn. It was an act of liberation.

It was the time of the Watergate scandal. Archibald Cox was appointed as the Special Prosecutor to investigate possible wrongdoing by President Richard Nixon and members of his White House staff.

Peter had been hired to work for Cox in the spring of 1973. That October was the Saturday Night Massacre, when Nixon tried to fire Cox for subpoenaing his White House tapes recorded in the Oval Office. The attorney general and assistant attorney general refused to fire Cox and resigned. Nixon's third choice from the Justice Department did fire Cox.

That created an uproar in the media and Congress. The following day, Sunday morning, all the lawyers who worked for Cox showed up at the Watergate office to protect their files, for good reason. Six months earlier, the acting director of the FBI, one of Nixon's henchmen, admitted to destroying evidence by throwing files he'd been given into the Potomac River.

I was at home that Sunday afternoon when Peter called and asked me to bring dinner in a picnic basket to the office. That's all he said, with no explanation. I drove to the office, with a full picnic basket, and discovered I was not the only Watergate wife with a hamper. There was a bevy of us.

An FBI agent was posted at each attorney's office door, and I was admitted to Peter's office after I opened the top of the basket for inspection. Peter asked me to stand at his desk, in front of his chair and face the door, and empty the basket. While I did that, he was busy stuffing files down the back of my slacks, under my trench coat.

When Peter was finished, he gave me a kiss on the cheek, and I went to the doorway, opened the empty basket for the agent to see, and tried to be cool walking with a load of files in the seat of my slacks. My heart was beating out of my chest as I waddled away to my car. I didn't remove the files from under my slacks until after I drove away.

When I got home, I put the files on top of the safe in our basement; when Peter got home much later, he locked them away. Twelve days later, congress appointed a new Watergate prosecutor, Leon Jaworski. Nine months after that, Nixon resigned. Beginning in 1975, the Watergate cover-up trial began, with all the evidence intact. I like to think that I played some small part for my country.

My marriage to Peter continued to unravel. I discovered that he was drinking about a fifth of bourbon a day, and the smell of alcohol oozed from his pores. He was drunk every night, and I couldn't stand seeing the man I loved kill himself, so I left. He was so drunk the day I signed the divorce agreement that his lawyer had to help him walk out of the room.

After that, I was an emotional refugee. I rented a room at a friend's home in Washington, and tried to dull the depression and confusion with marijuana. Basically, I stayed in a haze for about two years and finally snapped out of it when I moved to Chicago and got a PR job at the Ritz-Carlton.

Peggy died in May 1978. That's when my father sold

the newspaper publishing company and had to move to Florida for tax purposes. Dad didn't want to sell Shrine View and asked if I would live there. The timing was perfect. The Ritz-Carlton job ended when the hotel was sold, so I moved back to Pennsylvania.

The morning after Peggy's funeral, Dad and the five daughters gathered in the living room at Shrine View after breakfast. We were all sipping our Bloody Marys, while Dad handed out pieces of her jewelry. We laughed and showed off our new gems. Susan got the gold watch with the diamond-and-emerald bezel; Rosanne received the emerald and diamond ring (it wasn't the original platinum and diamond ring that Pop Smith had given to Granny. The original had been stolen.) Marjorie got a diamond pin; Betsy got the long strand of pearls; and I got a short strand of pearls.

No one mentioned Peggy's name. The eight-hundred-pound gorilla had left the building, and in fact, had left the planet. The mood was jubilant.

I had a flashback to when Dad's last dog died, when he cried openly about Misty's death.

"You're crying more about the damn dog than you'll probably cry at my funeral," Peggy snapped.

Well, she got that right. I didn't see a single tear shed for her, not by anybody.

Dad kept the housekeeper and the gardener at the house, and all I had to do was move my things in. What sweet irony: now I ruled the house from which I'd been banished twenty years earlier.

As for work, I was in the right place at the right time. The newspaper in Wilkes-Barre was having a strike. Even though the Smiths no longer owned the paper, I applied for a job. Because I was willing to cross the picket line and knew the town, the new owner hired me.

Armed with editorial experience at Time, I got my on-the-job newspaper training at the Times-Leader. I was back in the building I'd known since I was a little girl, when I visited my father at his office after school. Even back then, I loved hearing the roar of the printing presses and seeing the papers roll off the conveyer belt.

After a year and a half, my father sold Shrine View. It was the same time I made a quantum professional leap when I was hired at a daily paper in Washington, D.C. Even though I had been working as a copy editor, the editor was willing to give me a break as a features writer. It was my entree into writing, and the start of my writing career. When the Washington Star folded in 1981, I moved to Miami to another major metro daily, where I worked the night shift.

That meant I had no social life. I was dying of loneliness and started drinking alone when I got off work at 6 a.m. It was in Miami that I crossed the invisible line from social drinking to drinking alcoholically.

6 *1985*

BY 1985, I knew there was something wrong with my life, but I couldn't put my finger on it. When the house I'd been renting on Key Biscayne was sold, I moved into my father's place. He said since he was going to be away for six months (Nantucket and London), it would be helpful if I were there to look after things, including some redecorating. I was happy to oversee the work. Getting some new furniture and carpeting, having the place repainted and the kitchen retiled meant erasing the last traces of Peggy from the apartment.

There was a hitch about living rent free: I had to store all my furniture and send my two dogs to board with friends in Pennsylvania.

Even though I was drinking more, I still never drank before I went to work and didn't sneak drinks or hide my liquor. But my habit had changed. I used to drink one or two beers after work, but now I drank three bottles before going to bed. Even so, I was a fussy drinker. I bought only Canadian beer, and drank only from a glass, never from a bottle or a can.

At night I got up at eight o'clock, watched CNN to check the current news stories to be prepared for the office, showered, dressed and fixed dinner before driving to the newspaper, where I was a copy editor again.

My life was upside down and empty. I didn't have a boyfriend or any women friends. The few people I knew on Key Biscayne all drank too much for my taste, so I ended up drinking at home, alone. I preferred my own company to bad company.

One July morning when I got back home, I went to the fridge and saw I was out of beer. There was wine, but I drank wine only with meals. I went to make a Bloody Mary, but there wasn't any vodka, and the liquor store didn't open until nine o'clock. That was a couple of hours away. This was the first time I had a craving for a drink. I went to the liquor cabinet in the living room and grabbed the bottle of gin. I hated gin, the smell of it reminded me of Peggy. But that morning I poured gin to make a Bloody Mary. When I took the first sip, I felt a simultaneous repulsion and relief.

I held the second sip in my mouth before I swallowed and could feel myself make a face.

"Christ, I'm drinking just like Dad," I thought.

For years I had watched him make faces before he swallowed his liquor. I realized he'd been drinking when he really didn't want to, just as I was doing now. I went to bed at ten o'clock that morning and awoke with a terrible hangover.

By August I could feel myself unraveling and couldn't figure out what was happening. I thought a vacation in Pennsylvania would help.

I wanted to spend a week with my dogs, and to stay with my sister, Susan, who lived at Dad's cabin, about 30 miles west of Wilkes-Barre.

So I flew to Philadelphia, rented a car, and on the way to the cabin, stopped to visit with Richard, Betsy's college friend who had spent summers on Nantucket with us. That's when Richard told me about Susan.

"You might as well know, Ba, Susan's got a drug problem. She's actually been kicked out of a couple of bars for being so out of control and so drunk. I thought you better know before going out to the cabin."

I nodded without saying anything, stored the information, and left.

The next morning I picked up Patty and Buffy. It had been six months since I'd seen them, when Dad flew them to Pennsylvania with him and to board with friends. I started to cry when I saw them run toward me with their waggy tails and yelps of delight and kneeled for lots of doggie kisses. It was at that moment I vowed to get my life together in order to have my own place with my dogs.

When I got to the cabin and saw Susan, I was shocked. She was stick thin and looked so unkempt. This was a woman whose makeup was always perfect, with not a hair out of place. The next jolt was seeing that there wasn't any food, not in the fridge or the cupboards. I put my luggage in the guest room and drove straight to the market with her to stock up on supplies, including cat food.

When we got back to the cabin, I took the dogs for a walk along the stream that bordered Dad's property. When we were children, he used to take the five of us hiking out at the cabin, and we learned all the little paths and trails along the stream. That September day was glorious; the air was cool, the sun was out and the stream gurgled and bubbled.

When I got back to the cabin, I told Susan I was going into town to have dinner with Richard and see some friends.

It was about twelve-thirty when I got home. Susan wasn't in the living room, so I presumed she was asleep. I took the dogs out, came back to the cabin, and I went to sleep with Buffy and Patty on the bed with me.

I was awakened by the dogs' deep throaty growls, and it took a few seconds to get my bearings. I looked at my alarm clock, which read six. For a moment I thought it was six in the evening, but I saw the outside light and realized it was morning. That's when I heard voices in the front part of the house. I got up, put on my robe and went to the living room, and when I walked in, I saw Susan sitting at the dining table with two creepy-looking guys. There was a pile of white powder on the table, and the three of them were doing cocaine.

"What the hell is going on here?" I growled.

They all jumped in their seats and spun around.

"I want you out of here now, and don't come back the rest of the week while I'm here," I said menacingly.

The two creeps beat it out of the living room, and even before I returned to my bedroom, I heard the screeching tires on the dirt driveway. I also heard Susan's footsteps go to her room where she slammed the door. The pile of powder was gone from the table.

I fell back into a deep sleep, and when I got up, there was no sign or sound of Susan, and her bedroom door was still shut.

I needed to talk with someone, so I called Richard, drove to his house for breakfast and told him what had happened.

"I just don't know what to do, Richard."

"I know who can help you, Ba," Richard said. With that, he gave me the phone number of an old family friend who had stopped drinking.

I called George and told him about Susan. He'd been a classmate of hers, and his brothers and my sisters had all gone to school together, so I felt comfortable confiding in him.

George lived ten minutes from Richard's, and he invited me to drop by. When I got there, I told him about how shocking it was to see Susan so disheveled and hanging out with creeps. I also told him some of the stories I'd heard about her.

"I've heard the same stories, Barbara. The question is, do you want to do anything about it?"

"I'll do anything," I said.

He told me he'd been clean and sober for a couple of years, and that what had brought him around was a family intervention, which he explained.

"Do you want to do an intervention?" he asked.

"Yes."

With that, George put a plan in motion. He made a call to someone and then told me it was set for Thursday. I called my father and told him about the situation and that Susan was in a critical situation. I explained that George, whom Dad knew and whose parents had been good friends of his, had arranged for an intervention on Thursday and could he please come from Nantucket?

My father and Rosanne flew in, and a friend from Wilkes-Barre who had seen Susan's deterioration agreed to join the confrontation. The man conducting the intervention was the head of a local rehab, Marworth, in Waverly.

On Wednesday, we all met at Richard's for a practice session, and Nick Coangelo educated us about how interventions.

"Sometimes they work, and sometimes they don't," he said. "It all depends on the denial of the alcoholic. But taking action means you won't have any future remorse about not speaking up."

While we were talking and comparing notes, we discovered that Susan had been playing us each for a lot of money. She'd managed to cadge about ten thousand dollars in a little less than six months. She'd gotten the most out of Dad because she kept telling him that the reason she was having car accidents was to swerve from hitting a deer.

"It seems as if fifty percent of Pennsylvania's deer population has run in front of Susan's car in the last six months," the counselor said with a straight face.

The point of the intervention, Nick said, was to confront Susan about her behavior with love, not anger. He told us to write letters saying how we felt about how Susan looked and to mention the specifics of whatever had happened. He handed out paper and pens, and we sat at the dining table writing our letters. In about half an hour, we were ready.

"The point of this is to make Susan realize that she's not fooling anybody any more, that you will no longer enable her habit, and that you are doing this because you love her," the counselor said. "I'm going to have her sit here, on this side of the table, so she can't just bolt. And if things become heated, I'll step in and mediate so that this doesn't become a pissing match. That's not the purpose."

We all nodded and were collectively relieved that someone was in charge.

Nick had us read our letters and gave us feedback about some passages being too critical.

"Keep your remarks in the 'I.' Say how you feel about what you see and how you feel about her downward slide," he advised.

So we did our rewriting, and our re-reading, and he nodded with approval. We also decided to do the intervention at Richard's house

"It's also important that the element of surprise is on our side, that she doesn't suspect a trap. If she does, she'll run. Do you have any idea about how to get her here?" he asked me.

"Well, today she asked if she could borrow some money from me, and I gave her a twenty. When she learned I was going to the bank, she asked if I could get an advance on her Christmas money. I could tell her I arranged to get a check for twenty-five hundred dollars so she could make a down payment on a car," I replied.

"That's good. The money should bring her here. I'm going to set the time for one o'clock for all of us to meet here tomorrow. See if you can get Susan to come here by one-thirty. We can't count on anything, and if Susan doesn't show up, at least you know you tried to help her. And if something happens to Susan, at least you all know that you didn't remain silent, that you tried to do something for her. I've got a bed waiting at Marworth if she chooses to get sober," he said.

He looked at my father, and Dad nodded back and said, "Thank you so much for helping us."

The lure of the money worked. I told her that evening that the trust officer would give me the check tomorrow. I also said I'd give it to her at Richard's so she could get to the bank and cash it before closing time.

She agreed to meet me at one-thirty.

By the time I arrived at Richard's on Thursday, my father, Rosanne, George, Susan's other friend, Rick, and Nick were there. Nick told us to park our cars down the road and out of sight so that Susan wouldn't see a bunch of automobiles parked at Richard's. We reparked the cars, came back in and sat quietly at the dining table. At one thirty the phone rang. I answered, and it was Susan.

"Hi, I'm up at the mall and I lost track of time. So I'll be there as soon as I can," she said.

"Okay, I'll see you when you get here." But I wanted to make sure she got here sooner than later. So I added, "Susan, the bank closes at three, and I don't want you walking around with a check for twenty-five hundred dollars. So if you get here late, I won't give it to you until tomorrow."

I could hear her realize it was a now-or-never situation about getting the money today. "OK, I'm leaving now."

I relayed Susan's part of the conversation to everyone.

"That's very typical of an addict. The only thing predictable about an addict is the unpredictability," Nick said. "If she's really coming straight here, it'll take her about a half hour. I can't wait all afternoon since I've got appointments back at Marworth. If she's not here by two o'clock, I'm going to have to leave."

We all sat quietly. My heart was pounding and my hands were clammy and cold. Finally, we heard a car drive up, and everybody sat up. Susan walked in the front door, came through the living room and finally saw us when she got to the dining room.

"What's this?" she asked.

She was very cool and didn't show any surprise at seeing Dad or Rosanne or the rest of us at the table.

"Please sit over here, Susan," Nick said, and indicated a seat, the farthest one from the front door. She sat down, and once again asked in an even voice,

"What's going on? Hi, Dad," she added.

Nick spoke.

"Susan, your family is here because they're all concerned about you. Your father, your two sisters and two friends are here, and I'd like you to listen to what they have to say. When everybody's finished, then you can have your say," he said.

"Okay," she said quietly. She shot a glance at me and said sarcastically, "Thanks a lot, Barbara."

I cringed and felt guilty about betraying her.

Nick looked over at me and suggested that I start

"Dearest Susan, It hurts me so much when I see your physical condition. When I saw you at the cabin the other day, I was shocked to see how thin you were, to see you looking so messy. It hurts me to see that you don't have any food in the house to feed yourself or your cats. It hurts me to know that you've lied to me to borrow money, to say that you've needed it for one thing, but that clearly the money has been used to buy drugs. It hurts me to see that your choice of friends has deteriorated to the level of punks. It hurts me to know that I can't trust you. I'm telling you this because I love you and I hope that you will choose to do something else about the way you're living your life."

I started to cry when I finished and put my head down.

Dad read his letter next, and his voice cracked toward the end. He wiped tears away from his face when he was finished.

Rosanne read her letter and cried all the way through it.

Susan's friend Rick read his letter. And when he was finished, George spoke.

He didn't have a letter; he and Susan had known each other for thirty-six years, since they'd been three years old.

"Hi, Susan," he said in a friendly and even voice.

"Hi, George," Susan replied, smiling for the first time. Clearly, it was a relief that she wasn't going to have to listen to one more letter.

"Let me tell you about myself," George said. He kept his story short and direct about what had happened to him when he was using cocaine and drinking excessively, and what his life was like now that he was clean and sober.

When he finished speaking, Nick spoke.

"Susan, you have a choice. You can go to Marworth directly from here and stay there for four weeks. If you choose not to go, you have to move out of your father's cabin within forty-eight hours, and no one is going to send you money any more. No one is going to enable your addiction any longer. We all know what's going on. So the choice is yours," he said quietly and calmly.

Still cool as ever, Susan got up, looked over at Dad and said, "Sorry, Dad, I'm just not ready," and she was out of Richard's house like a flash. We heard a car speed out of the driveway.

I started to cry. Dad and Rosanne were silent. George and Rick left, and then Nick spoke to the remaining Smiths.

"Susan's got a disease, and I think you all would benefit from going to Al-Anon, the family support group for people who have loved ones who are alcoholics and addicts. Susan's very sick, and she needs help. And I urge you to keep your resolve about not enabling her drug use. If she telephones, ask if she's ready to go to rehab. If she says no, then hang up. I know that will be hard for you, Mr. Smith, but the more pressure you bring to bear, the better the chance of her hitting a bottom and being willing to stop. At least you confronted her with the truth today so that she can't lie to you anymore," he said.

Dad got up and said to no one in particular, "I'm going to ruminate for awhile." He went outside for a walk.

Rosanne left the room and Nick came over to sit next to me.

"Barbara, I don't think you need to go to Al-Anon. But I do think you're a candidate for Alcoholics Anonymous. Do you want to come to my office to talk about it tomorrow?"

I was stunned. What in the world prompted him to say that?

"Sure, I'll come to your office," I said.

That night, Richard, Dad and Rosanne were all very quiet at dinner. I had one vermouth cocktail before dinner, and nothing else. When I got back to the cabin, Susan was gone.

The next day at Nick's office, he handed me a list of twenty questions, compiled by Johns Hopkins University, to determine how alcohol was affecting one's life.

"Is alcohol a problem in your life? Don't answer these questions for me. Just answer them to yourself," Nick asked.

By the time I got to the middle of the typed page, I had a blinding moment of truth: Alcohol *was* a problem in my life. That summer I'd been editing the medical pages at the Miami News, and stories from the New England Journal of Medicine and the Journal of American Medical Association reported new research that alcoholism was genetic and that alcoholism was a dysfunction of the endocrine system, that alcoholics' livers don't metabolize alcohol in a normal function.

That's when I connected the dots. In a flash I realized that my father was an alcoholic, that I had a sister who was in A.A., and Susan and another sister drank alcoholically. I saw that I came from a long line of alcoholics. *I* was an alcoholic. I just never had the vocabulary to describe what I saw. This flash let me know what was wrong with my life and what had been plaguing me for months.

I looked up from the list of questions and said quietly, "Yes, alcohol is a problem in my life."

"How has it been a problem?" he asked.

"It impairs my judgment," I answered without hesitation, surprised at my spontaneous clarity.

Nick looked at me across his desk and said: "Alcoholism is like a downward elevator ride. You can get off on whatever floor you want. You don't have to wait for the elevator to crash into the basement," he said. "Susan seems headed for a crash."

I nodded and understood what he was saying without ever having discussed alcoholism before.

"The question is: Do you want to do something about it?"

"Yes," I said.

"There's at meeting at St. Stephen's tonight. And there's good A.A. in Miami. Good luck, Barbara. By the way, this is the first time I've ever run an intervention where the person who arranged it ended up catching the arrow," he said with a smile.

7 *1985–1987*

WHEN I GOT back to Key Biscayne, even before I unpacked my bags, I went to the fridge, took out all the beer and wine and put the bottles in a shopping bag. I did the same thing with the liquor bottles in the living room liquor cabinet and took the bags to the lobby and gave them to the doorman.

"I'm cleaning out the apartment, John. These are for you if you want," I said.

He looked in the bags, looked up and said, "Thanks, Barbara."

I also started a new routine. I went to recovery meetings before I went to work at 10 p.m. It was the start of changing playpens and playmates.

I also started dating, someone who was also newly sober. But I soon discovered that he had a hair-trigger temper. I felt like I was walking on eggshells and spent a lot of time trying to appease him after his outbursts. I was confused about what was going on, and I confided to a woman who had befriended me.

"I can't seem to end it, Kathleen. I vow to not to see him and then when he calls, I go mute," I said tearfully.

"Has he ever hit you?"

"No, but he raised his hand once, and when that happened, I quickly sat down on the bed and looked down and didn't say a word. As soon as he left the room, I grabbed my purse and ran out. I was afraid. I haven't seen him since."

The next day she gave me two books, "Women Who Love Too Much" and "Adult Children of Alcoholics."

That night, I read the "Women" book and couldn't put it down. Each chapter was a case history of women who were abused verbally and physically by their spouses or lovers. In each case, the woman had grown up in a household where the father was an alcoholic and where there was often a history of physical abuse. The stories told why the daughters gravitated toward alcoholic men. They were used to it.

I quickly saw my own pattern. While I'd never experienced violence, I saw that I'd been conditioned to verbal abuse and being hit by Peggy and that I had a tuning fork that propelled me toward alcoholic men, especially the bad boys—the charming ones who were inconsistent, didn't call when they said they would, didn't show up when they were supposed to, the Prince Charmings who were insincere. I also began to see how I ignored men who were nice, the ones who treated me well and respectfully.

The second book, "Adult Children of Alcoholics," left me stunned. When I finished, I sat and cried. It, too, illustrated how the patterns had been imprinted upon me. Long before my drinking started, the dynamic of growing up in an alcoholic household had left its mark. And because both parents were alcoholics, nothing was normal. I knew from the time I was seven, when I went looking for adoption papers, that it was nuts at Shrine View. My sisters and I called it "Shrine Zoo."

Everything was backwards. I was rewarded for lying, which I had to do in order to survive. I learned not to see the truth because it was too painful. I was punished if I told the truth. And if I related what I saw, I was told that what I had seen didn't happen.

"You saw no such thing. Do you need to have your eyes examined?" Peggy shrieked after I described her drunken behavior of lurching and staggering down the hall one evening.

I also learned not to count on anyone. There were countless times that Peggy and my father never showed up when they said they would, and countless times they would cancel plans because they were hung over. I got used to waiting in the cold or in the rain after a doctor or dentist's appointment because they were late. I learned not to trust.

When Dad got back from Nantucket late that fall, he

suggested I look around for a little place that he would buy for me.

"Do you mean it, Dad?" I asked, hardly believing what I'd heard.

"Yes. Get in touch with an agent and let me know what you find."

In about four weeks I found a place, and Dad kept his word and bought it. I was extremely grateful for his generosity; I was also grateful for the tax break that prompted his gesture. It worked out well for both of us.

The closing was on December twelve and, six days later, the house was cleaned, floors polished, all my furniture was delivered from storage, and I went into a nesting frenzy. I also had arranged to have Buffy and Patty flown to Miami.

I was ecstatic picking them up at the airport and taking them home. Finally, we were all together again, and all my belongings were under one roof. I was back in my own bed, the one that had been in Granny's "little girls' room" and my sweet dogs were lying beside me.

Before Christmas, I was let go from my job. That was a blessing in disguise. I was exhausted from working nights and burned out from reading on a computer screen for eight hours a day.

Not working meant I had a lot of catch-up time with the dogs after an absence of eighteen months. It also meant I had time to do a lot of reading about a new emerging field: co-dependency. After reading "Adult Children of Alcoholics," I wanted to learn a lot more.

Something I'd learned in early sobriety was a definition of insanity: doing the same thing over and over, expecting different results. For me, the pattern I wanted to break was being in bad relationships. And just as the drinking had been a downward cycle, so had my choice of men, most of them alcoholic. Now I wanted to change that.

That spring, PBS had a weekly television series about the dynamics of dysfunctional families. Hosted by John Bradshaw, it was the start of my education about emotional recovery, not just recovery from alcoholism. Reading the information was one thing, but hearing someone state, define and talk about the problem brought the information home on an emotional level.

Bradshaw claimed that one could break the pattern only after identifying it.

The new movement for adult children of alcoholics (ACOAs) happened in 1985. It was as if someone had thrown a collective lifesaver to an undefined group whose lives were desperate and lonely. I found an ACOA meeting and showed up one evening in May.

I'd been in a relationship with a man I'd met in meetings. But after ten months, it started to deteriorate. We'd begun with a sense of hope. He'd been sober for seven years and had also started reading the ACOA books. He even bought me the book "Fear of Intimacy," which we read together. We made a promise to be open and honest with each other.

In spite of his stated intention, he withdrew. I knew something was wrong, and when I asked him, he said "Nothing's wrong." He refused to talk. It's called stonewalling, and it was my first experience of being able to define and see a problem and to understand that my part was choosing someone who stonewalled.

I wanted to save the relationship, so I went to an ACOA meeting, hoping to learn something. About fifteen people were there, and I sat and watched and listened as people spoke. The therapist who was facilitating the meeting asked questions after people shared.

"What did you feel?" or "What's happening now?" she asked a couple of times during the meeting.

I'd never been in group therapy before and was fascinated to watch the dynamics of what was going on. Toward the end of my first visit, I was comfortable enough to take a chance and speak up. I explained that I'd been going out with a man for ten months and that he seemed to be backing off from the relationship but wouldn't tell me what was going on with him.

"I've written letters, I've called him and I get no response. I feel so frustrated that he's stuck in his process," I said.

"It sounds to me like *you're* stuck in his process," the therapist said.

"My God, you're absolutely right. I *am* stuck in his process," I said.

It was an ah-ha moment. I'd been reading about co-dependency but couldn't see how the dynamic affected me. I saw that I was more concerned about trying to control his behavior than taking note about what was going on with me. The nature of co-dependency, I was learning, was trying to control what other people were doing or else being a slave to what people thought about me.

The therapist's name was Cynde, and I noted that she never used a critical voice or tone, and she gave straight feedback. Or she'd stop someone by declaring "time out" in order to ask a question relating to that person's feelings. For the next six months, I went to this meeting weekly and got to know the regulars. I also got to know and trust Cynde, who recommended books to read. She also recommended that all of us become committed to the process of recovery by starting therapy.

I thought that my problem was only with my attraction to the "bad boys" and alcoholic men. I was aware that I had a habit of collecting wounded strays, as I called them. But I also started to see the bigger picture: my high tolerance for bad behavior. As a result, I had cultivated unhealthy relationships in every aspect of my life. I began to see how I neglected myself.

I also took note when Cynde said: "Not all co-dependents are alcoholics. But all alcoholics are co-dependents. And I encourage all co-dependents to get into therapy. That is recovery for co-dependency."

By the fall, I wanted to start individual therapy, but Cynde had no openings.

"Why don't you do some research, ask around and check out who else is available. And if you want to talk about your findings, feel free to call me," she said.

One of my inquiries led me to a therapist who was starting a sixteen-week course for co-dependents. After interviewing her, I signed up for the course.

Two weeks before the group was to start, someone gave me a tape made by Terrence Gorski, an addictions therapist. The tape dealt with the stages and tasks of recovery from alcoholism. One of the tasks was to stop all other addictive behavior—nicotine, caffeine, over-eating and workaholism. He stated that a continuing addiction impedes recovery. Although I'd stopped drinking alcohol, the spigot for nicotine and caffeine was still flowing. I knew I wanted the full benefits of recovery, so I was willing to stop smoking.

Gorski also emphasized the need for alcoholics and addicts to work on their family-of-origin issues by getting therapy. He emphasized that without help, people stay stuck in their old self-defeating patterns.

So I stopped smoking and went through five days of nicotine withdrawal—shakes, chills, fever, runny nose, diarrhea, coughing up balls of phlegm and having muscle spasms. In the middle of the fourth night I realized I was going through withdrawal. The next morning the fever had broken, my eyes were no longer watery, and I knew in my bones that I was an ex-smoker.

Later that fall, Rosanne called from Nantucket, where she was living year-round, to let me know she was coming to Key Biscayne for Christmas. I told her about my stopping smoking and also about the group therapy.

"Have you dealt with the physical abuse yet?" she asked.

"What physical abuse" I asked, and noted the irritation in my voice.

"All the physical abuse we got at home," she said evenly.

"Rosanne, I don't know what you're talking about," I said.

She didn't say anything else.

The new weekly group therapy sessions lasted for four hours, and after a month, the group was introduced to "anger work." The premise was that anger turned inward causes depression and that unexpressed rage keeps that person tied to the abuser. Releasing the anger in a physical way is literally "letting go." Since anger is energy, releasing it physically is the way to move it out of ourselves.

The therapists introduced us to batakas, foam-rubber bats about two feet long. The exercise is to kneel on the floor, sitting on one's calves, taking the bat with both hands over the head, then bringing it straight down onto a pillow with a lot of force and a scream of anger.

I was working in a group of four. When it came to my turn, I sat in front of the pillow and slowly raised the bat over my head, and when I started, I burst into tears.

"What's going on, DeWitt? What are you feeling?" asked Nicki, the therapist with our group.

"I'm afraid," I cried.

The moment I spoke, I had a flashback of Peggy raising a hairbrush and hitting me over and over. I started to tremble and could feel my body turn to ice. I started sobbing.

"I just had the memory of my stepmother hitting me,"

I gulped through the sobs. I collapsed on the pillow until the sobs ran out.

When I quieted down, I tried raising the battaca again, but again the tears came. I put the bat down on the pillow, feeling defeated.

"See if you can break through the tears, DeWitt," Nicki said softly.

That quiet encouragement was all I needed. Suddenly the image of Peggy looming over me and striking me on my back with a hairbrush propelled me to raise the bat, and I brought it down with a scream of rage I never knew I was capable of making.

Over and over, I raised the bat and screamed with anger. It had been stuck in my gut for more than forty years. It was the rage of a child who had been hit by a crazy, drunken woman, a woman who had it in for me, a woman who took out her rage and frustration on a helpless little girl. It was the rage I felt when I vowed never to give Peggy the satisfaction of seeing me cry. Through all those years of hitting, I never made a sound. I had forty years of silence to let out.

When I finished, I was limp.

Nicki put her hand on my back and leaned over and said quietly, "Good work, DeWitt."

I crawled over to a wall and put my back against a pillow. The exercise had left me in an altered state; I couldn't speak.

One of the women slid next to me and put her arm around my shoulder. I put my head against her and let myself be held.

When I got home, I walked Patty and Buffy and could feel myself still coming out of the experience. Even so, there was still a lot of energy moving around inside of me, more a feeling of agitation than anything else. The flashback had released the first memories of the physical abuse, and I was being flooded with them. Now I knew what Rosanne was referring to.

When I got back to the house, I went into the bathroom to brush my teeth. When I walked into the bathroom, I turned to the mirrored wall, saw myself raise my fist and say in a loud, angry voice: "What good did the goddam money and status do? We were supposed to be a privileged family, and it didn't protect me from a goddam thing."

A volcanic surge of anger flared and suddenly I was having a flashback. I was in my bedroom at Shrine View, lying on my bed reading. It was nighttime, and Peggy and my father were out. I heard the door open and it was Curtis, the houseboy.

He came into my room and closed the door and came over to my bed. "I want to show you something," he said, standing by the side of my bed. He unzipped his trousers and pulled out his erect penis. He took my head in his hands and said, "kiss it," and bent my face over his penis and tried to shove it in my mouth.

In a flash, I turned my face away and lay down on the bed on my stomach, and covered my face with my hands. "Show me how you play with yourself, Barbara," he said gruffly. I lay on the bed without moving. Then I heard his zipper.

"Get up," he snarled. "Get under the blanket."

I quickly got under my covers, and he leaned over and put his face next to mine.

"If you ever tell anybody I was here, the devil is going to drown you in your own blood. You will die if you tell. Do you understand? Do you promise not to tell? If you break your promise, the devil will kill you," he hissed.

"Do you promise?" he asked insistently.

I was terrified. "I promise," I whispered.

He left the room, closed the door, and I was afraid to turn out the light. I was afraid to close my eyes.

I had never heard the word penis but now I knew what one looked like without even knowing what it was called. I was seven years old.

8 *1987*

I WAS SHOCKED by the memory. My raised fist went limp and dropped to my side as I stared in the mirror. Until this moment, I'd had no idea that I'd been sexually molested.

This was no trick of my imagination; the details were vivid and clear. The memory was like a movie film, with every frame in focus and the words spoken clearly.

I could feel the terror all over again remembering the words, "the devil will drown you in your own blood."

Just as swiftly as the Curtis memory emerged, a second one came. Now I knew, forty years later, why I ran into the closet to hide when I'd heard Curtis's voice in the kitchen at Shrine View when I was seven.

My whole body felt sick, and I turned to the toilet and threw up. When I was finished, I washed my mouth, brushed my teeth and used lots of mouthwash to get rid of the foul aftertaste.

But my mind had been fouled by the memory, and I couldn't sleep. By the end of the next day I was operating in a daze. I'd stop in the middle of a sentence and couldn't remember what I was talking about; I'd arrive someplace without remembering driving there; I'd stop mid-task unable to recall what I was doing.

I went to Cynde's regular weekly group. I was feeling very remote, and when I spoke, it was as if someone else were speaking. I felt physically disconnected.

When I sat down, I said I had something important to share and I recounted the events of the previous night.

Cynde spoke.

"I want you all to take a good look at DeWitt. Look at her eyes and listen to how flat her voice is. What you are seeing is a person in dissociation," she said.

I heard her, but it was like a long-distance voice. The room got very quiet, and I looked around and saw everyone looking at me like a piece of evidence. But I couldn't feel a thing, not even self-consciousness.

"I feel I've been in a white-out in a snow storm," I said.

"I want you to be careful when you drive home tonight, DeWitt. Try not to drive unless you absolutely have to," Cynde said.

In about ten days, I came to. I can't remember any of the particulars except I knew I shopped for food and walked the dogs.

I do, however, remember the day I snapped out of it. Around noon, my doorbell rang, and when I opened the gate, my neighbor was standing there with a dog in her arms.

"Good morning, Barbara."

"Good morning, Brenda. Is this your new dog? You've already got three boxers," I said. I smiled at the sweet-looking creature.

"That's precisely why I'm here, my dear," Brenda said in her crisp English voice. "This little stray followed my maid here from the Metrorail station, and I can't allow him in the yard. Bandit would tear him apart. I've called the animal control officer, and he's supposed to be here in a half-hour. I just thought I'd check with you to see if you want another dog."

Bandit, her alpha boxer, patrolled her yard ferociously, barking at anyone who walked by the iron fence.

I stared at the dog and then back at her.

"Oh, thanks for making me the only thing standing between this dog and the gas chamber. If I don't take him, you know bloody well I won't be able to sleep for weeks," I said.

I put my hands around his little muzzle and stroked the top of his head. His coat was rust and white and smooth, and he was the size of a small beagle with terrier ears. He gazed up at me with an adorable dog look, and I knew he was mine.

"Well, put him down, and let me see him," I said.

Brenda put him on the grass, and I leaned over.

"Hi, there. Aren't you cute?" I said.

He wagged his tail as I looked at his collar and saw his rabies tag.

"Brenda, he's got a tag, you know."

"Yes, I've already called the Dade County Dog Tag Bureau, and they gave me the name and number of the vet who distributed that tag," she said efficiently.

"I don't suppose you happen to have that information with you right now," I asked with a laugh.

She gave me a sheet of paper from her pocket and said, "As I matter of fact, I do."

"Patty and Buffy aren't going to like this at all. And neither is Miss Puss," I said, referring to my eight-year-old cat. "Well, I'd better buy him a lead and give him a bath."

"What are you going to name him?"

"Hmm. George. I'm going to call him George," I said.

"Oh, I like that. Well, George, you're a lucky boy. You've

got a good home," she said. "Thanks, Barbara. I knew I could count on you."

I closed the gate and said, "Come on, George."

The dog, who was thin and dirty and had been a stray until a few minutes ago, trotted up the walkway as if he owned it. Before I got to the front door, I dashed inside to get a dog lead to put on George. Patty and Buffy, who'd been lying on the back deck, came ambling in, and as soon as they saw George, their hackles went up.

"It's all right, Patty. We've got a new dog here and the three of you are going to have to work it out," I said.

She came over and sniffed George, then Buffy did the same thing and to George's credit, he didn't bark or growl. He joined the sniffing ceremony, until he spied Miss Puss sitting by the chaise. He bolted over to her, but she didn't move, and when he got too close, she took her paw and swatted his nose. He yelped, backed off, and I never saw him bother her again.

George went to the groomer's that afternoon and cleaned up nicely. That night there was a shift in the sleeping arrangements. Patty and Buffy stayed in their doggie beds, and George and I became bedfellows.

During the four-month group therapy, I was astounded to learn that most of the men in my life had been like my father. That shocked me since I'd gone out of my way to find men who were not like him. I'd even gone out of my way to marry men as ethnically opposite as possible. Burt was the "Russian Jew," and Peter was half-Czech, half-Indian, born in Moscow.

The men didn't look like my father and weren't in the same profession. What I didn't realize was that I was responding to their emotional interiors, men who were critical and dismissive.

The role I perfected was that of the listener, which came from Harrison's "Listen to me, listen to me" command after he'd had a few cocktails. So I learned to pay rapt attention and fix an adoring gaze. Invariably, most men told me, "DeWitt, you're such a good listener."

"Listen to me, listen to me" became another of my father's phrases that my sisters and I joked about. In therapy, a new meaning started to emerge. My brain had its own translation: If I listened hard enough, maybe a man would love me.

During the four-month group therapy, I met a lawyer and started seeing him. There was a lot of sexual flirtation and energy between us, and one night after dinner we went back to his house. The kissing got hot and turned into foreplay, and I finished undressing in his bedroom. He was already undressed and in bed. As he watched, he said, "Oh, red tights. I've never fucked an elf before."

The remark made me laugh. I got into bed and found out right away that he knew his way around a woman's body. There was no talking as we started moving. It had been about seven months since I'd had any sex, and I felt a rush of raw sexual energy. I was moving as usual, and suddenly, a whole new thing was happening. My voice started to moan, a sound from deep inside, not just from my throat, and I felt myself letting go and getting lost.

"Don't stop," I moaned.

"Don't worry, I won't," he said.

And it started all over again.

When the floating was over and my breath was coming back, I realized I'd just had my first sober orgasm with a man. I was overwhelmed. Equally overwhelming was the thought that I never knew that I hadn't had one before.

"Was I drunk or so high on marijuana that I didn't remember having an orgasm? Were all the others just fake orgasms?" I wondered. Maybe that was the truth. I wasn't sober enough to remember.

Whenever I masturbated, I had an orgasm like the one I'd just experienced. I saw how much I'd been shut down sexually, that I shut down just before a climax. It was like taking the ride up the roller coaster track but never going to the top.

"This is the first orgasm I've ever had with a man," I told him.

"Whaddya been doing? Having orgasms with women?" he asked.

"No, you jerk. It's just that I've never had one with a man before."

He wasn't the least bit interested in my revelation.

I lay in bed thinking about my own sexual history. Obviously the trauma with Curtis had affected me without my ever knowing it. Some part of my brain thought it wasn't safe to have an orgasm.

Now I understood why I usually had a couple of drinks after sex. It helped put out the fire of sexual frustration that I felt.

"Isn't it odd that I loved so many men and couldn't have an orgasm with them, and here I'm having orgasms with someone I don't love at all," I thought.

Then my partner propped himself up on his elbow and purred, "I'd really love it if you let me use some handcuffs, DeWitt."

His suggestion threw me off guard.

"No, my dear, I don't do handcuffs, not unless they're sterling silver and from Tiffany's," I replied, in what I thought was a sophisticated brush-off.

"I can't get them from Tiffany's, but I sure as hell can get them in sterling silver. Just tell me yes," he said, all excited. He took my wrists in both his hands, put them over my head by the headboard, and said throatily, "You'll love it."

He was serious.

"I was just kidding, Carl," I said.

"Let me know if you change your mind," he said as he let my hands go and rolled over to go to sleep.

That scenario was grist at Cynde's that week. When I told the group about the handcuffs and making the remark about "as long as they're sterling and from Tiffany's," I thought it would bring a good laugh. But no one laughed.

"What prompted you to say that?" Cynde asked.

"I thought it was brushing him off," I replied.

"It doesn't sound like a brush-off to me," she said.

And then my friend Barbara spoke up.

"The remark says that abuse is okay as long as it's wrapped pretty or comes with money. That's the story of your relationship with your father. And, in fact, all the men in your life," she said quietly.

That truth was stinging, and I started to cry

I never saw Carl after that. I was relieved but agitated. The orgasm door had shut as quickly as it had opened.

The rest of the spring was a collision course between my past and my present. After the ACOA group ended in February, I was having trouble getting my bearings after all the emotional discoveries, and I had no way to take the edge off—no alcohol, no cigarettes, and no sex to medicate myself. The old escape hatches were closed, and there was nowhere to hide from my feelings.

After years of thinking that men were the problem in my life, I was beginning to see the truth about some of my women friends. Therapy showed me that I chose just fair-weather friends, nobody I could count on. With Peggy as a role model, no wonder the women I knew were cavalier and sarcastic.

I saw how I had replicated the dynamic of neglect.

Working on the family issues in therapy was very different from reading about them; it was the difference between reading about how to ride a bicycle and actually riding a bicycle. The reading was informational; the therapy was experiential.

What kept me going was discovering that I wasn't alone. The other people in the therapy group were sharing their own traumatic revelations. I got to see how children growing up in an alcoholic family were left with deep, invisible wounds. What I was also learning was that I didn't have to stay in the system of neglect or abuse. The message was clear: divorce the family of origin and create a family of choice. But divorces can be messy, especially if family members are in active addiction.

The role I had played in the alcoholic family, as first-born, was the hero/caretaker. Because of Peggy's alcoholism and daily pill popping, I assumed the role of the caretaker at an early age whenever there wasn't a nanny around. By the third grade, when I was seven, I was making sure Marjorie and Susan were up and dressed for school and that at least we all had toast or a piece of bread before we got on the school bus.

I was also learning to decipher the unspoken codes. For instance, "Children should be seen and not heard" meant I didn't have the right to question or speak up. That was the "no-talk" rule.

"Think of those poor starving children in Korea" my father would say. Peggy used that as emotional blackmail to force me to eat food I didn't like. She kept me seated at the dining table for hours after everyone left. I sat there crying and gagging, trying to swallow cold food that I found unbearable, like turnips, or Brussels sprouts or creamed onions. I didn't dare express my rage at her cruelty for fear of being hit.

"Don't ever embarrass the family name," was code for not talking about all the insanity I witnessed. Drunken neighbors would arrive at all times of the night, mostly on weekends. My sisters and I never knew who would be sleeping in the other twin bed in our rooms. One night, I saw a very drunk Peggy dragging an even drunker state supreme court justice in an arm lock across the street to his home, both of them screaming at each other. The next day, as the grown-ups drank their Bloody Marys, they laughed about how "snockered" everyone was night before, as if nothing has happened. Another laugh about a "bad boy."

When I was about ten, one spring Saturday afternoon, a neighbor was having an outdoor ladies luncheon. After Peggy had walked across the street for the gathering, I saw my father go up into the attic and emerge shortly in one of Peggy's old maternity dresses and wearing a hat with a draped ostrich feather. He put a pocketbook in the crook of his arm and ambled across the street in a pair of bedroom slippers.

I followed him at a distance and watched, fascinated, as he went to the back lawn where the women were sipping whiskey sours. I stood behind a hedge and watched his entrance, complete with a grand falsetto.

"Well, how do you do? I'm Mrs. Magilacutty, and I just moved into the neighborhood, and I didn't think you'd mind if I dropped by for cocktails," he said in a faux English accent in falsetto.

I'd never seen a man in drag before, and the sight of my father sitting down in a dress and lady's hat with rouge on his cheeks had my eyes bulging. All the women were laughing and one of them handed him a whiskey sour. He raised his glass and said, "Cheers."

Even though I knew it was theater, I also had the distinct feeling that a lot of people would find it weird to see the newspaper publisher dressed in women's clothing sipping cocktails on a spring afternoon.

No matter how much I tried to keep a poker face during any of Peggy's rants, sometimes tears came anyway. And she would screech: "You ungrateful child. You have the best money can buy. Take that look off your face or I'll get the hairbrush. Then you'll really have something to cry about."

The anger work and crying revived these painful memories. In the morning, when I sat to meditate, the tears started and all I could do was give in to the sadness. My eyes were red from so much crying. And the voices that had been silenced by my drinking sprang back in my head. Something was happening, but I didn't know what. I lost my appetite and was afraid to go to sleep. I didn't feel safe until the sun came up. Then I'd sleep for two or three hours. My body was starting to feel like lead, but my mind was wired. The voices just wouldn't stop.

During the day I kept busy answering ads for jobs and sending out resumes. But I had no responses.

When I was first out of work, I took a course in sketching and water coloring at the Miami Art Museum. Now every afternoon, I sat on the back deck to draw and paint, and that seemed to suspend the turbulence. But the anxiety about running out of money and not being able to pay my bills started the replay of Peggy's relentless berating.

"What's the matter with you? Are you stupid? You're forty-six years old, unemployed, can't get a job, can't seem to hold a job, and can't get your life together. You're a failure.

Who'd love you? You're an ugly little girl. You're a miserable, ungrateful girl. You'll be lucky if a truck driver marries you. If only you were dead, this family would be perfect."

One morning after only two hours of sleep, the voices in my head were all competing at the same time, and I couldn't hear anything except "if only you were dead." I couldn't stand the pain and confusion.

Suddenly, a single thought quieted everything: "I'll kill myself."

I wouldn't have to feel any more pain, and all I had to do was drive to South Miami to buy a gun and bullets. Finding a gun store was easier than getting a parking space at 7-Eleven.

The next thought was "What about my pets?" The current count was three dogs and two cats.

"I'd rather kill them than leave them orphaned for the pound," I thought, and I visualized what I had to do.

"I'll take the cats—Miss Puss and Rudy—into the bathroom, and kill them first, a clean shot to the head for each one. Then I'll corral the dogs and kill George, Patty and Buffy in that order. I'll do Buffy last because she's deaf and won't know what's going on."

When I visualized putting the gun to my own head and pulling the trigger, I started to sob, but couldn't see any other way out. The pain was unbearable.

I brushed my teeth and dressed. "No point showering. I'll be dead in an hour," I thought.

9 *1988*

ON THE WAY out the front door, the phone rang. I looked at my watch. It was just eight o'clock. The phone rang again, and out of force of habit, I turned around, walked back into my bedroom to answer it.

"Hello?"

"DeWitt. It's Barb. I just got the most terrible feeling about you. Are you okay?"

Barb was my friend from Cynde's group. I was very silent before I could get my voice to work.

"No. I'm going to kill myself. I can't stand it anymore," I whispered.

I could hear the flatness of my voice as I spoke.

"DeWitt, promise me you won't do anything. Just sit down by the phone and I'll call right back. Do you promise?" she asked.

"Yes."

"Tell me you promise, DeWitt."

"Yes, I promise, Barb," I answered.

I sat down and stared out the window at the avocado tree in the center of the backyard.

In a minute, the phone rang again.

"Hello?"

"DeWitt, it's Cynde. Barb just called me, and she's worried about you. What's going on?" she asked.

"I'm going to kill myself this morning. I'm on my way to get a gun. I can't stand the pain any longer. I'm going to kill the animals, too."

When I heard myself say that, I started to sob.

Cynde waited until the sobbing stopped.

"DeWitt, can you come to my office at noon? I've got appointments I can't cancel, otherwise I'd see you right now. Can you hang on until then?"

I thought about it for a few seconds.

"Yes. I'll come to your office at noon," I said and hung up.

I started to cry again and tried to speak out loud, but words wouldn't come, just babble. My thoughts were all jumbled and nothing was making any sense. The noise was at full pitch.

"I'm going crazy," I thought.

I looked at my watch; it was eight-fifteen.

"Christ, three and a half hours before I leave for Cynde's," I said out loud. I was surprised to hear myself say something rational.

I got in the shower and stood under the hot water. Tilting my head back under the shower head seemed to expel some of the mumbo-jumbo. When I got out, I felt calmer and headed for the kitchen for a cup of tea. I got my morning paper from the front yard and took my tea outside to the deck off the kitchen. By now, my little coterie of pets had followed me; they all settled into their favorite spots and stretched out, including the two cats. I'd acquired a new cat last month when a friend left him with me.

"It's a good thing Barb called, or we'd all be dead ducks by now, darlings," I said to the pets and smiled at my macabre joke.

My next thought was a sobering one.

"Oh, Christ. If I commit suicide, that means I'm going to have to come back and deal with being an alcoholic and having alcoholic parents all over again. Oh, shit. I might as well get it all over with this lifetime," I thought.

I took a deep breath and knew I'd make it to Cynde's at noon.

I finished my tea, walked the dogs and then stretched out on the leather couch. George jumped up by my feet, and Patty and Buffy stayed on the floor.

I was able to nap before going to Cynde's office, and when I walked in and sat down, she got up and closed her door.

"What's going on with you, DeWitt?"

I started sobbing again and reached for the tissue box on her desk.

"I feel like I'm losing my mind and that I need to be locked up in a psycho ward in a padded room. Nothing's making any sense, I'm going crazy," I stammered.

She waited for me to catch my breath before speaking.

"DeWitt, you're not going crazy. You're in crisis. Do you want to do something about it?"

"Yes, anything," I stammered.

"I'm going to call Chit Chat," and she flipped through her Rolodex, picked up the phone and dialed.

Chit Chat was the informal name for the Caron Foundation, a rehab in Pennsylvania that also had a residential program to treat adult children of alcoholics.

"I've got a patient in crisis," she said, "and I want to register her for the residential COA program," she said.

Hearing Cynde say "in crisis" let me know where I was on the emotional map.

"Uh-huh, I see. Can you hold a minute?" She put her hand over the phone and said, "Their crisis list has a three-week waiting list. Can you hold on that long?"

I looked at her and laughed, "A three-week waiting list? Oh, I see, suicide hotline, please hold. Yes, I can hold on. That'll give me some breathing room from the edge of the cliff."

She smiled and nodded and returned to her phone. She asked for an available date, wrote it down and hung up. She then gave me the piece of paper with all the needed information.

"How about joining me for some lunch?" she asked.

Over our meal, she suggested I go to a lot of A.A. meetings for the next three weeks, two or three a day if I needed to, and to keep calling people.

"Why don't you come to the Highland-Park meeting tonight?" she suggested.

"Okay, I will."

"Be sure to call me if you need to, DeWitt," and she gave me a hug before I parted.

By the time I left, the thought of killing myself had evaporated. Now that I knew I wasn't going crazy, I had a sense of hope. I drove home and slept for a couple of hours. When I woke up, I called my friend Kathleen and told her about what had happened today.

"I don't know how I'm going to pay for it, Kathleen. The five days at Chit Chat costs $700. I don't have any money, and my father's in Europe and won't be back until the twenty-seventh. I can't ask him for money until then, and I'm supposed to be at Caron May twenty-ninth."

"DeWitt, I'll be glad to pay the tuition. Just tell me the date you need to go, and I'll call them to say I'm sending a check for you," she said softly.

I was dumbfounded by her generosity. "Oh, Kathleen. I don't know when I can ever pay you back."

"I'm not worried about it," she said.

At six o'clock, I headed over to Cynde's meeting and sat in the corner, where I just cried. The tears wouldn't stop.

Cynde spoke up right away.

"I want everyone to go over to DeWitt, one at a time,

and softly massage her shoulders and neck for about five minutes," she said.

During the hour and a half meeting, one by one, everybody came over. I was so grateful for their gentle touches, and touched even more when each person leaned over and said, "I love you, DeWitt."

I was having a breakthrough. I didn't care how I looked or what anybody thought. The facade had cracked, and I had no energy to preserve it. Nobody in this group had ever seen me cry, and I felt great relief in not giving a damn.

"So this is what being emotionally authentic is like," I thought.

When I got home, even though I was exhausted, I still couldn't sleep. So I just read until dawn. At least the noise in my head had stopped. When it started to get light outside, I turned off the lamp and fell asleep.

The next day I got a free-lance writing assignment, and for the next three weeks, during the day I interviewed people, wrote my stories and delivered my assignments. At night I went to meetings and read until dawn.

Once my father got back from Europe, I had to deal with him before I left for Caron. I dreaded having to ask him for money—it made me feel like such a failure—but I had nowhere else to turn.

Too afraid to face him, I wrote a long letter and explained what had happened, that I'd had "a breakdown," the same thing that had happened to him back in 1954. I told him about going to Caron for a week of therapy to deal with the issues of the sexual abuse and physical abuse. Then I asked if he would lend me some money. I ended by saying that I was feeling too fragile to see him and that I would call him before I went to Caron.

The next day, I phoned and went to see him.

"Hi, Dad."

"Hi, Barbara. How are you?" he asked, and I saw him reach for my letter, which was on the table next to his chair.

I went over to the couch and sat down without saying anything.

He looked perplexed and said softly, "I got your letter, but I don't understand everything you wrote. What sexual abuse and physical abuse are you talking about?" he asked.

When I started to cry again, I realized he'd never seen me cry, let alone break down and sob. When I caught my breath, I told him that Curtis was the one who molested me, and then I told him about Peggy's beatings.

He said, very quietly, "Barbara, I had no idea. I just didn't know."

When I told him about my needing money, he said, "Of course I'll give you the money. I'll call the bank in the morning. I'll write a check for you now and have the bank send you a check."

"Thanks, Dad. Thank you so much," I said in a whisper and hugged him. For the first time in my life, I felt his genuine concern about my well being.

Two days later I left for Caron, which is tucked away in the hills of southeastern Pennsylvania, just outside of Reading. The building had been a hotel after the Civil War and was used as retreat from the summer heat of Philadelphia. It sits atop a hill lined with towering, shade trees, and the place is quiet, and the air is clean.

I walked into the registrar's office and sat down by her desk.

"Your name?" she asked.

Oops. The voices went off in my head again, at full volume. I couldn't think straight.

"Should I call myself Barbara because that's my first name? Should I say DeWitt because that's what everybody calls me? Did Kathleen send the check in for Barbara Smith or for DeWitt Smith? Am I here to do the work for Barbara, the little girl, or am I here to do the work for DeWitt, the one whose life is falling apart?"

The debate inside my head confused me, and I started to cry.

The woman at the desk looked up at me and said gently, "That's all right, dear. We'll come back to that. What's your address?"

It was a relief to answer a simple question and I stopped crying to give her the rest of the information she needed. When she returned to the name part, I said, "Barbara Smith."

By nightfall, twenty-seven of us had registered, and we met in the living room after dinner. By ten-thirty, I headed upstairs, got ready for bed, got into bed and for the first time in more than a month, felt safe enough to sleep. I slept for eight hours.

The following week introduced me to the experience of emotional recovery. In five and a half days, I had fifty hours of group therapy, basically a year's worth of therapy packed into one week. All of us had had our personal breakthroughs.

Everyone was there because of a crisis that could no longer be put on hold. The mere act of showing up at Caron was a step out of denial to admit there was a problem.

Our big group was broken into three groups of nine, where we did our personal work, including anger work with the bataka bats. One morning one of the therapists was lead a guided imagery. We all lay on the floor, eyes closed, and listened to the instructions for an image we were asked to conjure up in our minds.

"Go back to the house where you grew up, and enter the front door," said the therapist.

That's all I heard and when I came to, I heard the therapist say, "Now take your child out of the house and walk away knowing that you are safe."

I had fallen asleep during the entire exercise. The therapist turned up the lights and everyone sat up slowly. I became upset about falling asleep, thinking that I'd done something wrong. I immediately went over to the therapist and told him what had happened.

"It's all right, Barbara. You didn't do anything wrong," he said gently. "Maybe it wasn't safe for you to go into that house and you were protecting yourself."

Another huge truth revealed.

"There was nowhere in that house that was safe for me. In fact, it burned down seven years ago, after my father sold it. And when I drove to look at the ruins, all I could think of was how much I hated that house and that I was glad it had burned to the ground," I told him.

He nodded.

"So you were taking care of yourself by not going into that house," he said.

During the week, I also learned a lot about anger, mourning and psychodrama. It was all a process of healing. Mostly I learned that I didn't have to suffer alone anymore. By week's end, my counselor gave me two things. The first was a piece of calligraphy that read: "You are important." The second, she whispered: "You are lovable."

I had the "You Are Important" calligraphy matted and framed and have carried it with me all the many places I've lived since Caron. It's the first piece of art I hang on the wall whenever I move to a new home.

10 *1988–1990*

BACK IN MIAMI, it was time to put Humpty Dumpty back together again.

I didn't have the emotional stamina for a full-time job, so I found a part-time job and worked from five until midnight. By the time I got home and walked the dogs, it was one o'clock in the morning, only four hours until sunrise. Although I had no trouble sleeping at Chit Chat, I found I couldn't sleep at night when I got back to Miami. So I read until sunrise and fell asleep on the couch in the living room.

By fall, Cynde had an opening in her private practice. At first, I was nervous and self-conscious because individual therapy was different from working in a group. I soon found out that I didn't always know what was going on with me. Cynde helped me see my dilemma or conflict.

The first problem was the issue of not being able to sleep. Now that the head noise had died down, I saw what my nightmares were about—Peggy and Curtis coming into my bedroom. No wonder I was still terrified to fall asleep at night. It was the fear of intrusion I'd been carrying around since childhood, not feeling safe once I got into bed.

Working with Cynde started to change that.

"When you get into bed tonight, I want you to visualize Curtis in a cage in your bedroom, wherever it's safe enough to put the cage. I want you to examine the cage and know that it's impossible for him to get out. Do that every night for a week and see what happens," she instructed me.

That night I did the visualization exercise. I put the

cage in the far corner that I was facing. When I realized he couldn't escape, I fell asleep and slept through the night. It was the first time in eight months that I'd fallen asleep at night in my bedroom.

The next night I did the same visualization and placed the cage in the same corner. I was amazed to see that the cage and Curtis were smaller. He had shrunk to midget-size, and the cage was tight around him. Cynde didn't give me any instructions about shrinking him, it just happened. I kept my eyes closed and fell asleep, again facing the direction of the cage. For the second night, I slept the whole night through.

On the third night, the cage and Curtis were minuscule, smaller than an inch. Again, I had a peaceful sleep.

The fourth night, nothing appeared. It all went away.

The next night I started over again, but with Peggy in the cage. And the same downward progression happened in the same number of days.

When I saw Cynde the following week, I told her what happened. The experience showed me why I'd been such a light sleeper and why I'd always slept facing the bedroom door.

By autumn, I found a job as a receptionist at a classical radio station. Work was easy, the office was light and airy, the people were nice, and listening to classical music all day was wonderful. Whenever a string piece played, such as Tchaikovsky's Violin Concerto or the Brahms Violin Concerto, I was moved to tears. One morning the program director came out of his office and saw me cry.

"DeWitt, how glorious," he said, with his hands raised upward. "You're the first receptionist who's understood this music."

I smiled and put my right hand over my heart, and he nodded at me and said, "Carry on, DeWitt, carry on."

I didn't tell him I was in therapy and just about anything made me cry.

The surprise that year was my father's remarriage. One day in late May when I stopped by to visit him, he said coyly, "You know, Dorothy and I are getting very serious."

He'd been dating Dorothy for three years. Since the Smith family tends to speak in code—being in therapy certified that—I asked him point-blank, "Does that mean you're going to get married?"

"Well, we might," he said, still being vague.

My brain went into overdrive.

"Well, Dad, the only reason I ask is to suggest you get a prenuptial agreement. If her two unmarried children want to go back to school and she asks you for the tuition, that means you'll have to touch principal," I said, knowing full well that would push his Republican button.

He put both hands to his forehead as if a fire poker had just branded his temples, and he said in absolute horror in a raised his voice, "Touch principal? Touch principal? You know we *never* do that."

I refrained from smiling at his predictable reaction.

"Listen, Dad, here's the name of a good lawyer I know. He's a partner at a law firm and does this sort of work. He's expensive, but it's worth protecting the estate from situations you can't possibly be aware of," I said.

I wrote out the name and number of the attorney.

"That's a very good idea, Barbara. Thank you," he said.

Dorothy and my father were married in June, and they went to Europe for a wedding trip before going to Nantucket for the summer. I knew she genuinely cared for my father and that he'd stopped being so terribly lonely since Dorothy had come into his life. For that, I was very grateful. I gave her a very personal wedding gift, a Mark Cross passport folder with her new monogram imprinted. She was touched when I gave it to her at their wedding luncheon, where it was just the three of us.

I knew that my relationship with my father was about to take another shift. It had taken a huge shift when I stopped drinking, since we no longer sat and talked and drank together. It certainly took another shift when I moved out of his place. And now that he was remarried, it was shifting again. I got a glimpse of just how fast three days after they had left for Europe.

I drove out to Key Biscayne to get some of my things that were still at Dad's. I let myself in with my own keys and walked into the living room, where I came face to face with Dorothy's twenty-one-year-old son.

"Hi, Barbara," he said, and then he introduced me to the man sitting on the couch.

"This is my father, and he's staying here for a couple of days," he said. "I'm living here for the summer," he added.

I shook hands with his father, who just nodded. He never stood up to introduce himself. He didn't say a word.

"How do you do? I'm Barbara Smith and I'm collecting a few of my things," I said in a reserved tone.

I knew his name was Paul Welborn, a misnomer by what I saw.

It was enough of a surprise to find Daniel all moved in. But his father? Dad and Dorothy had left for a European honeymoon just the previous day. What cheek that Dorothy's ex-husband was staying there. I had the feeling that my father hadn't been told about this, and the lack of propriety was a little appalling,

This was the apartment that my sisters and I had used

freely since Peggy's death eleven years ago. It was also an apartment we all thought we'd inherit. That picture was changing, fast.

"Looks like her children are in, and his children are out," I thought.

I got my things and checked for my mail on the hall console. In addition to my mail, I saw an open envelope from a law firm. I looked inside and pulled out a bill to my father. It was an itemized bill for adding Dorothy's name to the deed of the apartment.

I also had to process Daniel's announcement about his being at the apartment all summer.

That meant I'd lost the use of the place. I was used to driving out to the Key to swim on my days off and using the apartment to shower and change and have some lunch on the balcony. That was out now.

But there was more. Daniel also told me his mother had given him the keys to my father's Rolls-Royce to drive in order to keep the battery from going dead.

"Christ, move right in and move right up," I thought.

Driving the Rolls-Royce in my father's absence had been my privilege. I loved driving the Rolls. Not only was it magnificent to drive, but also it was a right-hand drive, which made it a novelty. And it's true: After driving a Rolls-Royce, everything else is just wheels.

This was a lot of information to take to my new therapy group. This group had come together a year after I got back from Caron. Everyone in the group was a recovering alcoholic, and we had all gone to ACOA treatment over the past year. Cynde agreed to lead the group.

Everyone there was committed to change. A main element for me was to learn how not to internalize feedback as criticism. The feedback was essential because I had a blind eye about myself. I had no idea how I presented myself to others, and learned that I wore a mask. My mask of cool was a defense mechanism, and it prevented me from being authentic or real.

Because Cynde was there to keep the group on track and have us work on issues as they arose in each session, I felt safe trying out new skills. I learned to be honest and direct instead of being silent. I learned that withholding was a form of dishonesty and stonewalling.

The group work also taught me that revealing myself was a form of healing. I was able to push through the silence and the façade and discovered I was terrified about being honest.

At Caron, I learned that my primary aim was to protect myself and take care of my needs, and it was going to take time and practice to learn. Cynde's group was the place to practice because it was safe.

Peggy's volcanic rages made me vow I'd never to be like her. So I kept my anger in check. As a result, my anger resided in my jaw, and over the years, I had ground my four back teeth so hard that my jaw ached when I woke up. Eventually, I ground my back teeth to the point where they had to be extracted.

Whenever any doubts arose about whether therapy was working, all I had to do was look around the room to see how it was working for everybody else. The results were visible.

The nine of us became very close. Doing all that intimate work allowed me to experience the "family of choice" principle that I learned at Caron. I discovered that I had the option of choosing a family, people who were kind and trustworthy

In individual therapy, I was dealing with the abandonment issues that came from not having a mother in my life. In group therapy, I was learning how not to be critical of myself and others, not to channel the voices of Peggy and my father that were implanted in my brain. I also came to see what a perfectionist and how rigid I could be. This became apparent when Cynde gave me the assignment of not making my bed for a month.

"You can change the sheets, but don't make the bed," she said.

The first couple of days it drove me nuts to leave the house with the bed unmade. I could feel my body twitch with the compulsion to go back to make it. The exercise also let me see my habit of unconsciously choosing to be late for an appointment rather than leave a few dishes in the sink. Messy things literally got under my skin. My whole goddamn childhood had been so messy; no wonder I'd tried so hard to keep my little room neat as I could. It was the only control I had over a messy life.

By the end of the second week, Cynde asked me to keep the Sunday papers strewn on the floor by my chaise. Normally I left them in a neat and tidy pile on an ottoman. Leaving the papers in a messy array on the floor made me want to scream. Again, I was willing to follow Cynde's direction, to learn how to be flexible.

Sometimes I asked her, "How long is this going to take?"

"As long as it takes," she replied.

The process of removing my mask—the front I'd hidden behind all my life—was painful. It felt as if the mask was pasted on with super glue, and taking it off left me feeling raw.

"You're climbing out of a deep, deep, dark hole, DeWitt" was what Cynde kept telling me.

The hardest thing was learning to express my anger. First, it took time to identify the fact that I was feeling angry. And when I learned it was safe to be angry, I didn't know how to express it appropriately. I'd only seen raging. Peggy had held the whole family emotional hostage with her insane anger. We all walked on eggshells to keep her from blowing up. Deep inside, I was terrified of expressing my anger because it meant being punished and hit. My job was to break through being shut down. I also saw that when I got angry, I cried because I didn't know what else to do. They were tears of frustration, not sadness.

"Push through the tears, DeWitt," Cynde would say.

Finally, one day during a session, I cried out in rage: "Nobody ever protected me."

"No, DeWitt, no one was there to protect you. Now you have to learn to protect yourself," she said.

11 *1990–1991*

CYNDE GAVE ME the emotional support while I was digging my way out of the deep, dark hole. I learned to trust her since I knew there would be no criticism or humiliation.

Another objective of therapy was learning to get rid of the critical voices that had been implanted.

It was frightening to see how I unconsciously channeled Peggy's voice, years after her death. I had to stop that inner voice and replace it with a kind, loving one.

With no role model of a loving mother, I was clueless about how to be kind and loving with myself. I had to learn to mother myself.

My history reminded me of something Charles Dickens wrote, citing the orphan's words in "David Copperfield": "I had no advice, no counsel, no encouragement, no consolation, no assistance, no emotional support of any kind."

Another issue was the matter of feeling worthy.

Being punished and constantly being told "no" killed any sense of being worthwhile. For instance, when I went to boarding school, I asked if I could take riding lessons.

"No," Peggy yelled. "Do you think money grows on trees?"

I was confused. The fact is I saw live-in help, a big house, trips to New York, Europe, Jamaica in the winter and Nantucket in the summer, and a constant round of cocktail and dinner parties and dinner-dances. Peggy went to New York at least once a year to shop. And my father, who was basically indifferent to fashion, nevertheless had two tuxedoes—one for summer and one for winter—a pair of tails and a morning coat, which he wore to both my weddings. He also loved shoes and had dozens, including a pair of dress pumps with grosgrain bows that he wore for dinner dances. It never occurred to me that riding lessons would be a financial hardship. But the subtext from Peggy was: "You're not worthwhile."

But this time, her "no" was a pivotal moment. For the first time in my life, I wasn't taking "no" for an answer. I discovered I could outsmart her. When I got to school that fall, I asked the headmistress if I could earn money in exchange for riding lessons. It turned out I could by working as the night receptionist for all the incoming calls, after the office help had gone for the day, and Granny paid for my riding clothes. That was a huge victory for me, especially when I won a blue ribbon for the jumping class I competed in at the annual Horse Show.

Cynde gave me another exercise: to meditate on a photograph of myself when I was five years old. It was a head and shoulders portrait in an old silver frame. I had a little Dutch bob—bangs and straight hair to below my ears. Friends always told me that it was a beautiful photograph. But I couldn't see it because all during my childhood, Peggy said, "That haircut is awful. You look so ugly."

It wasn't until I went to Caron and started therapy that I brought the photograph out of a box it was stored in for years after Shrine View was sold.

Cynde's instructions were: "Just look at her and see what happens. Try to make contact with that little girl."

Every morning I sat on the floor, meditation style, with the photo about four feet away. With my eyes closed, I visualized the image and imagined little Barbara seated across from me. The first time I did the visualization, the little girl had her head down and refused to look at me.

I did the same thing all week, with the same results. When I went to Cynde's the following week, I told her what had happened.

"DeWitt, you abandoned your child years ago, and she doesn't trust you. Give it time. It will take time for her to trust you. But it's important that you reach her," she said.

Cynde gave me my next set of instructions.

"Every night, draw before you go to bed," Cynde said.

"Draw what?" I asked.

"Draw whatever your hand draws, not your brain," she said.

So I bought some crayons and drawing paper and sat on the deck and let my hand draw like a child.

Six weeks later, I brought all my drawings to a session, and she showed me all the things the artwork told her. This was my introduction to art therapy. My little-girl figures were always standing alone and apart from everything and everyone else. And always, I stopped the figure at the waist with a tight belt, or stopped the figure at the shoulders. Cynde said that these were strong indications about being sexually molested, that I was cut off from my body from the waist or neck down.

Another aspect of the therapy was to not blame. While there were things that happened to me as a child, it was my responsibility as an adult to correct the wrongs. I was responsible for the corrective emotional experience. That meant dropping old behaviors and learning to replace them with healthy, new patterns.

It meant letting go of being a victim. Because I had been conditioned to bad behavior and had a high tolerance for it, I was learning to say no, and that "no" was a complete sentence..

Cynde also taught me how to accept compliments. Whenever I was complimented, I had a habit of brushing it off or discounting it. Even when someone offered to help, I rejected that by saying, "No, don't bother. I'll do it." And when the Caron therapist told me I was lovable, I cried. It was incomprehensible, and yet, that's what I wanted the most: to be loved.

"To be loved, you have to love," Cynde would tell me. "And to love, you have to learn to love yourself."

"I feel so unloved," I replied.

"I love you, DeWitt," she said.

Hearing that made me cry. It was incomprehensible.

She told me to get the book, "Learning to Love Yourself" and suggested that I get massages regularly so that I wouldn't feel touch starved. She knew I was low on cash and told me about a massage school that offered clients very low prices in exchange for the massage students to practice.

I ended up with a standing weekly appointment at "Educated Fingers" for an hour's massage for fifteen dollars. The experience taught me how touch starved I was and that it left me emotionally anorexic. I didn't know how to take in physical nourishment; getting the massages was a start.

I also started doing little things for myself, like putting flowers in the house. I didn't have to buy any in lush semi-tropical Miami. I just picked them when I walked the dogs. During gardenia season, my house was filled with the sweet fragrance of those beautiful white flowers that grew outside my front door.

By now, I was working again, as a reporter for the Key Biscayne weekly newspaper. When the editor left six months later, the publisher asked me to be editor. I said no, thank you. The next day at Cynde's I told her that I'd turned down the job.

"What's the matter, DeWitt? Are you afraid of success?" she asked.

That was a wake-up question. We spent the rest of the session discussing how I sabotaged myself if no one else was around to do it for me. When I got back to the office, I told the publisher I'd love the job.

The job was wonderful. The staff were all women, from the publisher on down. I'd always worked in a newsroom dominated by men, and this was an entirely different atmosphere—not the push-push, shove-shove testosterone energy. It was the first time I experienced a collegial office.

At one session, Cynde told me to give myself a "sick day."

"I want you to ask different people to come to your

house all day long to do things for you," she instructed. "Ask someone to fix you breakfast, someone else to fix you lunch and someone else to fix dinner. Have someone walk the dogs for you and read to you. I don't want you to do a thing. Just stay in bed."

So I made a list of women I'd grown very close to over the past two years and felt comfortable enough to ask for their help. Actually asking them was still difficult, but I did it.

All of the women said yes and chose their two-hour shifts. On the appointed day, I slept until nine, got up, showered and put on a fresh nightie, and got back into bed. Cathy was the first one to arrive, and she fixed breakfast and brought it to my bedroom on a tray with a fresh flower. While I was eating, she walked the dogs. When she returned, she took the tray, did the dishes and came back to sit with me.

I felt very uncomfortable having anybody wait on me, but I stayed in bed anyway. Cathy and I had known each other for three years. She'd gone to Caron and was in Cynde's group as well. We laughed and talked softly, and she gave me a hug when she left.

When Susan arrived at noon, I was a little more comfortable. She sat on the bed with me and we chatted until she made lunch, which she brought to the bedroom on a tray. After lunch, she cleared away the tray, and she gave me a hug when she left.

My dear friend Barb arrived at two. We'd known each other for almost four years, ever since I'd joined Cynde's hospital group. We'd spent hours together, at the beach, going to the Miami Book Fair, having meals at each other's homes and walking our dogs. She had three Dobermans, and when we took our dogs to the Key to walk, we looked like professional dog walkers: two women with six dogs.

Barbara's task was reading. When I got back from Caron, I bought a beautifully illustrated copy of "The Ugly Duckling." I read it over and over again, and when I got to the part about the emerging swan that had been rejected all its life, I would cry. That was the book she chose to read.

And when she finished each page, she held up the book so I could see the engraved colored illustrations. And when she got to the next to last page, I reached for the tissues and started to cry. The part that always gave me a shiver was the picture. It showed a beautiful bird emerging and discovering itself for the first time.

She read the last page, closed the book and reached for my hand and held it, just the way Granny used to do when she finished reading to me. How poetic that today I was lying in the same "little girls" bed from Granny's house and remembering my grandmother. Barbara gave me a hug, closed the mosquito netting that encased my bed, and I sank into my pillow and slept.

Diane was the last handmaiden on the shift. She fixed a light supper for me, and we talked afterward. By the time she left, it began to sink in that I could receive without giving, that I could be loved without having to perform.

At my next session, Cynde asked about the experience.

"It was wonderful," I said.

"And how did you feel?" she asked.

"I felt loved," I said.

Cynde's message was clear: Establish a new family, a family of choice. Establish a support system of people who love me, instead of repeating the family of origin who were constantly critical or neglectful.

"The alcoholism made it impossible and makes it impossible for them to understand emotional needs, yours or theirs. It was the same with your own alcoholism. You didn't know your own needs—physical or emotional—when you were drinking. And you're still learning. The messages you got were all fucked up."

12 *Spring 1991*

AFTER LIVING IN South Florida for almost ten years, I got the itch to move back north, especially after the dermatologist who was treating me for skin cancer said, "You know, your people came from a cloud-covered island. That's where you should be living, not in the place that has the highest rate of skin cancer in the U.S."

Well, I had a house to live in on Nantucket, most certainly a cloud-covered island. Once the idea of moving to Nantucket took hold, there was no stopping me.

When I told my told my father, he asked, without a trace of sarcasm, "Barbara, you're leaving a very good job where you're respected in the community, leaving a house where you don't have to pay rent to go where you don't have a job and where you'll have to share a cottage with your sisters. I must say, I don't understand."

I was touched by his fatherly concern.

"To tell you the truth, Dad, it doesn't make any sense to me either. All I can tell you is that I'm following my heart," I said.

I packed my clothes and a few things I didn't want to leave behind. My plan was to rent my house furnished, and Dorothy said she'd take care of finding a renter. Against my better judgment, I let her handle it. Her over-eagerness raised my suspicions.

But the convenience overshadowed my suspicion, and I violated my instinct. So I left all my belongings—the furniture, rugs, kitchen things, books, pictures—without having to put everything in storage.

I rented a six-foot U-Haul and filled it with my clothes, papers, television set, stereo, computer and my bed, the one from the little girls' room. I couldn't bear leaving it behind.

The Subaru station wagon was also packed full, with barely enough room for the three dogs. I hated leaving this little house in Coconut Grove, this place I'd had lived the longest since I had left Shrine View. After moving around for years, it had been a luxury to have the same address and phone number for five years.

Before I drove away, I walked around the house for one last look at all the furniture, most of which had been at Shrine View, and before that, at my grandmother's home. There was the teak partners' desk with inlaid leather that my grandfather had gotten in the Philippines during the Spanish-American War, and the nineteenth-century mahogany Sheraton sideboard that had been in my grandmother's dining room. I had my own acquisitions, such as a cream-colored Italian leather couch for the living room, a chaise in the study and two rosewood bookcases. I looked at all the art, a lot of it Granny's oil paintings. Hardest to leave behind were my books. I'd packed two boxes; there simply wasn't room for the rest.

Walking around reminded me of that day a year ago when my house was robbed and the thieves took all of my grandmother's silver and what little bit of jewelry I had.

As soon as I discovered the theft, I called the police and then phoned a friend who was a cop on Key Biscayne. I knew him because I went to the Key police station to get the police report for the paper. Gordon was at my front door in about ten minutes. He was on duty and still in uniform and gave me a hug when I answered the bell.

"Are you okay, DeWitt?"

"No, I'm feeling very shaky, Gordon. I'm so glad you're here," and I started to cry.

"Tomorrow, you're coming to the gun range with me. I'll give you a nice little Smith and Wesson thirty-eight, something you can handle, and you're going to learn to use it. No arguments, DeWitt," he said.

When the Miami cops arrived, Gordon said: "You take good care of my friend here," and he drove off in the Metro-Dade police cruiser.

I put the three dogs in the backyard and then let the police in. One cop immediately started dusting with his brush and powder on the sideboard where all the silver had been.

"You're lucky, Miss Smith," said the cop who'd been taking notes. "The woman across the street was hit by these two black guys just before you left your house this morning. They broke in, pulled her out of the shower, pistol-whipped her and stole all her money, silverware and jewelry. She's lucky she wasn't raped. But she ID'd them from the mug books at the police station this afternoon. They're crack addicts with long rap sheets," he said. "I can tell you, your stuff has already been fenced and melted."

"You want my advice? Get a gun. If you hear any noise in your yard, just start shooting. Nobody in Miami's gonna charge a nice white lady like you for protecting yourself," the Cuban-American cop said.

The next morning, a contractor arrived to fix the fence where the thieves had gotten in. Then I left to meet Gordon at the shooting range. Before I got into my car, I saw my neighbor who'd been pistol-whipped. Debbie's swollen and bruised face was visible from across the street.

I walked over to her to give her a hug.

"You're so lucky you weren't home, DeWitt," she said.

Seeing her doubled my resolve to learn how to use a gun, and I vowed no intruder was going to come into my house and threaten me.

Gordon was waiting outside the gun shop.

"Hi, sweetheart. How ya doing?" he asked and he leaned over and kissed my cheek. "Before we go inside, I wanna ask you one question. If you have a gun, do you think you're capable of firing it if you need to?"

"After what happened yesterday, yes," I replied with no hesitation.

The thought of Granny's antique silver and sterling flatware being fenced at a crack house and sold for nothing made me furious.

"You'll never find it, honey, so don't even put out the effort," Gordon said.

He bought a box of one hundred shells, and I put on the eye glasses and ear protectors. We went to a cubicle where he showed me how to load and empty the revolver. Then he made me load and unload the gun several times. He'd also bought ten target sheets, which showed the head and torso of a man. The bulls-eye was over the heart, and the concentric circles beyond that had numbers for tallying the score of the bullet hits.

Gordon clipped the first sheet on a wire that looked like a clothes line and, by a push-button control, sent it out into the enclosed range. He stopped the target when it was about forty feet away.

"Plant your feet, hold the revolver like this," he said and showed me a two-handed grip. "Then aim. Look through the sight at the end of the barrel, put your target in the center of that, take a breath and squeeze the trigger smoothly," he said.

I took a deep breath, pulled the trigger, just like he said, and saw the bullet pierce the sheet. The noise startled me, but I got used to it after emptying the chamber. Then I settled into aiming slowly and seriously.

Gordon pulled in the first sheet, sent the next one back into the range. By the third sheet, all the shots were staying within the bulls-eye circles and hitting the target in the torso.

When I emptied the box of shells and Gordon held up all the sheets, he said, "Jesus, DeWitt, remind me never to call you a cunt when you've got a gun in your hand, will ya?" he said. "You're a regular Annie Oakley. You're all set, sweetheart."

I smiled at his cop humor.

He gave me a box of bullets and the Smith and Wesson with its zippered leather case; I got in my car and drove off. When I got home I loaded the gun and put it in the top drawer of my night table, next to my spiritual books. I laughed at the juxtaposition. "Heaven and earth co-existing," I thought.

When I moved to Miami eight years ago, my intention was to find a job and a man. Instead, I found sobriety, a therapist and sober friends. Living by the ocean and under the palm trees had helped my healing. Now it was time to head north, back where I belonged.

I had three days to get the ferry, which meant driving five hundred miles a day. My heart sang with every mile I headed up I-95. When I reached Providence, Rhode Island, I bore right.

Patty was up front with me, and George and Maggie in back. The driving time was brainless. The only time I had to think was when I parked, to make sure I could pull out of the parking space without having to back up and jackknife the U-Haul.

I was thrilled to cross the Florida border and leave behind the unbearable heat, humidity and the goddamn fleas. By the end of the second day, it was cool enough to turn off the air-conditioner and roll down the windows to smell the cool air.

The drive allowed me to reminisce about all my dogs. I got my first one after my first divorce, a sweet, black continental-sized poodle, whom I named Smudge. Next was Sure Shot, a four-month-old liver-and-white English springer spaniel. Sure Shot and Smudge were great companions, but I had to part with Smudge when Sure Shot had a surprise coupling in Central Park and got pregnant. I hated giving up my sweet little dog, but she went to a family in Scarsdale who had a big yard and a summer house on Fire Island. When Sure Shot had her litter, I found homes for six of the pups when they were two months old and kept one. I gave Sure Shot to friends on Nantucket who'd been looking for a springer spaniel. The puppy I kept was named Bright Eyes. When I remarried, Bright Eyes was part of the family, and when I divorced, my ex-husband demanded custody of her. It broke my heart to give her up, but my life was too unstable to keep her. Giving up custody of my three dogs over a four-year period broke my heart, and after Bright Eyes, I vowed I'd never again give up a dog.

I love and adore dogs. Oh, God, I love the smell of dog in the morning! It's so reassuring to wake up with a dog on the bed. When I moved back to Shrine View, I got Patty and Buffy, two springer spaniels and it was glorious to have dogs again after a six-year absence. In Miami, George and Maggie joined the group, Maggie being a hundred pound Labrador retriever mix who was abandoned on Key Biscayne.

The day I had to have Buffy put down, Cynde came to my house and held me while I sobbed. Buffy's death marked an important rite of passage for me. I'd had her for her lifetime, which meant I'd kept my vow about not giving up another dog.

When I got to Hyannis, I headed straight for the dock to be first in line for the afternoon boat. When I finally drove onto the ferry and took the three dogs to the upper deck, I could smell the saltwater and delighted in the squawking gulls. Seeing people dressed in sensible Yankee clothes—not an inch of Spandex anywhere—and hearing conversations only in English reminded me I was home.

The boat left the dock, headed out into the bay and finally into Nantucket Sound. Two hours later, I spied the bluffs of Nantucket and went out on deck to watch as we moved past the Brant Point Lighthouse, built in 1746. The gold-leaf steeple of the Unitarian Church and the rest of the town's silhouette were backlit against the five o'clock sun. I was elated.

When the ferry was docked, I drove off the boat and slowly over the cobblestones of Main Street, and headed out to 'Sconset to Codfish Park and pulled into the driveway. The dogs and I got out of the car and ran down to the beach.

"Hiya, Ba."

I turned around and saw Betsy on the deck with her dog, a wolfish-looking hound who came streaking down to inspect the three new dogs on his turf.

"Hi, Betsy," I yelled and waved. She walked onto the beach, where we hugged.

"Blue, Blue," she called to her dog. "You behave yourself."

The four dogs were deep into their sniffing ceremony, and then in a flash, Blue and Maggie went running up the beach together in playful zigzags. George and Patty were busy sniffing out the property as Betsy and I walked into the house.

"I'm here, dogs and all my worldly possessions," I said.

13 *Summer and Fall 1991*

I settled into the smallest of the three bedrooms, the one with the single bed. That first week, I painted the walls, had curtains made with material I'd brought from Miami, hired a carpenter to build some bookshelves, scrubbed the floor and furniture with bleach and water and then did a sage ceremony to chase away any traces of Susan's drug and alcohol binges (she'd spent the last two summers in this room).

I hung my clothes and pieces of art, placed my little objects and books on the shelves and put down a rug. I also put in the two L.L. Bean dog beds for Maggie and Patty, and George slept with me.

I was so happy I'd brought my own linens and towels since the things in the linen closet were from Shrine View.

The next task was getting my own mailbox and telephone line. Everybody else—Dad, Dorothy, Betsy and Rosanne—shared one mailbox and the same telephone number, which meant it could be days before mail or messages reached the right person. After a week of feathering my nest, the next task was finding a job at one of the weekly newspapers, but there were no openings. Even so, I managed to get two free-lance writing jobs on one of the papers, but that was it.

When I left the Miami News, where I had worked overnight for years, I vowed I'd clean houses before ever working nights again. Now it looked as though that pledge was about to come true.

Betsy owned and operated the 'Sconset Cleaning Service, and I ended up working for her. I also got a morning job delivering The New York Times and the Wall Street Journal in 'Sconset. My world had turned upside down. A month ago, I was paying someone to clean my house; now I was cleaning other people's houses. A month ago I was the editor of a newspaper; now I was delivering newspapers. I felt like Alice who'd fallen down the rabbit hole.

The first time I left with Betsy for a cleaning job, I felt mortified. The job was opening a small house, and when I got on my hands and knees to clean the toilet and scrub the bathroom floor, I felt so defeated.

The next day she gave me a job directly across from my grandmother's old house, where I'd spent my summers as a child. As I drove there with a Saks Fifth Avenue shopping bag full of cleaning rags (my Saks bags used to hold newly purchased clothes), I had a piercing thought: "Oh, God, please don't let me run into Edward."

Edward was the man I'd been engaged to, literally, the boy next door. His family's house was next to Granny's, and I'd had a crush on him when I was a little girl. We met again in the summer of 1969 when we were both in 'Sconset the same weekend. He was lean, handsome, had great green-gray eyes, an easy laugh, and was smart. When the weekend was over, he gave me a lift back to New York, where we lived three blocks apart. We dated that entire summer. During the week, we saw each other in Manhattan and on weekends we went to Nantucket and stayed at his mother's. One weekend, his mother came into the guest room when I was getting ready for bed, and said to me point blank, "Barbara, please, please marry Edward."

I assured her that if Edward asked, I would marry him. I was crazy about him. A year and a half later, he did ask me to marry him, but ten days before the wedding, I broke off the engagement. I'd been standing in the 'Sconset chapel with the florist, talking about the floral decorations. Suddenly my body went numb, and I couldn't feel anything.

That's when I realized I couldn't go through with the wedding. I started to faint and caught myself on a pew. And I flew back to New York despite the wedding being following week.

When I got back to the apartment where Edward and I lived, the first thing I did was grab a bottle of bourbon, run upstairs to our bedroom, sit on the floor in the corner, twist off the top and take a few swigs. I'd never drunk straight from a bottle, but I needed to get up my nerve to tell Edward I was backing out.

I was desperately confused and had no one to talk with to help me sort out my thoughts and feelings. If only I'd had a mother to talk to. If only I had known enough to go to a therapist. But I'd had no one.

By the time Edward arrived home, I'd brushed my teeth and made myself presentable. Although I didn't have the courage to tell him the whole truth, I said I'd gotten cold feet and couldn't go through with the wedding then. Would he be willing to postpone it? He was so kind and under-standing, which made me feel all the more guilty.

Equally awful was having to make the phone call to Peggy.

"What?" she screeched. "The invitations have gone out, I've made all the arrangements at the club, the flowers have been ordered. For God's sake, Barbara, why can't you go through with the wedding? You can always divorce him later."

For a split second, I actually thought about doing that, but in my heart I couldn't. I told Peggy I was afraid that Edward drank too much.

So the wedding was postponed, Edward took off for France and used the reservations we'd had for our honeymoon. I was back on the shit list and estranged from the family again.

The real reason I couldn't marry Edward was because I was having an affair with his best friend. Peter and I were married six months later, and eight months after that, I discovered that he was hiding a whiskey bottle in his bureau. I realized the folly of my choice and saw that I'd been a fool.

I'd stopped drinking the summer of the swigging incident. It scared me to realize I was drinking too much. Even at my wedding I didn't drink any Champagne. It was when we were in Big Sur for a vacation that Peter promised he wouldn't drink. But one day when I was putting away the laundry, I discovered the hidden bottle of bourbon.

My body turned cold, just like the day in the chapel, and I thought, "Oh, my God, I married the wrong man. Peter's the one with the drinking problem, not Edward." A year and a half later I left Peter. By that time, he was drinking a fifth of bourbon a day and packing a bottle in his briefcase to take to work each day.

The marriage was awful. Peter worked late every night, and whenever the phone rang, I was terrified that it would be a call saying he'd been in a car accident. Nightly, he arrive home drunk, fix a drink, and not say a word until he passed out in the bedroom. The marriage was dead sexually and emotionally. The one time I got up enough nerve to say, "Peter, you're drinking too much. Can't you please stop?" his reply was a growl: "Stop nagging me."

Night after night, I stayed up late, chain-smoking cigarettes and joints, crying and not knowing what to do or where to go for help. I had no idea the problem was alcoholism. That was in 1973, and I hadn't heard anybody use that term. I defined the problem as Peter "drinking too much."

I kept asking myself, "Where did I go wrong?"

I thought I'd done all the right things: married the Harvard lawyer, had had the right jobs, had the right, stylish clothes, did the right things, and I was miserable.

As I pulled up to the house on Sankaty Avenue, I looked over and saw a car pull up across the street. Then I saw Edward step out of the car. We hadn't seen each other in 18 years, and there we stood facing each other across the street. I called his name and went over to him.

When he saw who it was, he held out his arms and embraced me. I stood in his arms for about a minute, and moved away for fear I'd start crying.

Edward looked down at me and said warmly, "Come on in and meet my wife."

"Yes, I'd like that," I said, forcing a smile.

I entered the house where I'd spent so many happy days and nights, so very long ago. Now Edward and his wife and their children spent their summers there. They lived on Nantucket year 'round, and lived in town during the winter. I made a hasty exit after looking at some photographs and catching up on news about his family.

I ran across the street to the house I was supposed to clean and burst into tears.

"Is this what my life has come to?" I cried out.

The deep remorse and sadness about leaving Edward swept over me. That one impaired choice, to sleep with Peter, had deprived me of all the things I desperately wanted: a husband, children and a loving home of my own. When I was done sobbing, I finished the job and returned to Codfish Park, where I made an icepack for my swollen eyes.

"Why the hell did I ever sleep with Peter in the first place?" I asked myself angrily.

"Because I'd been drinking," I said out loud.

Oh, my god. That was awful truth about my alcoholism: it impaired my judgment. I'd made that blurry choice when I was drunk and high on pot. I'd gone off with Peter because he stayed up late drinking the way I did. Although I'd stopped drinking for a couple of years while we were married, I'd taken up smoking marijuana. My life with Peter was a haze of pot, which I smoked to escape the reality of my unraveling marriage.

What was also stunning was to realize that it had taken me six years of being sober before I saw the truth. The fog sure lifted slowly.

The next day, I was still in the midst of my emotional hangover, when I got a call from my father, who was still in Key Biscayne.

It was his habit to start speaking immediately, without saying hello, how are you, not even a "Hi, Barbara." Today was no different.

"I've got some news. I've sold the Coconut Grove house, and you have to empty out all the furniture by the end of June," he said coldly,

I could feel my body start to shut down.

"But, Dad, what happened? I thought the house was rented for a year. What are you talking about?" I asked.

"No, Dorothy's tenant backed out, and so we put the house on the market and sold it."

It turned out her tenant was her 21-year-old son, the one who lived in the Dad's apartment that summer he married. Goddamn Dorothy. I *knew* I shouldn't have trusted her. She'd only been interested in finding housing for her son, not helping me. Sneaky, sneaky Dorothy.

"Dad, can't you please store the furniture? They're the last of the things from Shrine View," I pleaded.

"No, I'm not going to store another goddam thing. You'll simply have to empty out the house. The new owner is moving in July one," he said and hung up.

I felt like screaming, but all I could do was sob. I had just been told to get rid of all my possessions, the last things I had to my name.

It was bad enough that last year I'd lost all of Granny's silverware in the Coconut Grove robbery, but this loss was everything—my art, books, and furnishings I'd collected since my divorce twenty years ago. I'd left that marriage with my clothes in two suitcases and had been a gypsy for five years until I'd moved back to Shrine View. That's when I started working again and could afford to buy new books and clothes and some art.

The next morning I called the Miami Herald to run an ad for a house tag sale, then called a friend to ask if she'd do the tagging for me. I told her she could take whatever furnishings or items she wanted plus ten percent of the sales. Diane agreed to help me.

The day of the tag sale, Diane called to tell me how much had been made, and how little the big pieces had sold for, and how she'd saved my baby book from being thrown out. Somebody at the tag sale had lifted the bench seat in the study and discovered the books that I had stored there that I'd forgotten about. Diane retrieved the old pink book, the one in which my mother had recorded my birth and the events and clippings of my first year, the one I used to read in the attic in Shrine View.

"I went through it, DeWitt. It's so loving with all those notes and Valentines your mother pasted on the pages. I'll send it to you," she said.

"Thanks, Diane, for helping me out in a pinch. I love you," I said.

I hung up and took the dogs for a walk to cry to myself. When I got back, Betsy was in the driveway, saw how upset I was and gave me a hug.

Rosanne was standing in the driveway, too, and was dead cold. She didn't offer a kind word. Nothing. Just like her mother.

I got through the next few weeks because Betsy turned a few small rental houses over to me. That meant I could work my own hours, alone, just pack up my cleaning caddy, my Saks rag bag, my three dogs, two Tabs and my peanut butter sandwiches, and off I'd go. I adopted the attitude, "If I've got to sweep floors, then I'll be the best floor sweeper there is." It helped.

In a couple of weeks, my body rhythm changed. I got up early to deliver the papers on my paper route, and after breakfast and a run on the beach with the dogs, I showered, dressed and drove to the house of the day. The next four or five hours of cleaning were like a workout. I liked the physical work and could feel my body become more limber after years working at a desk.

My Brazilian jazz tapes got me through a lot of bathrooms and kitchens. When I finished, I rounded up the dogs who hung out on the front porches, headed back to Sandpiper for an afternoon swim and then a long nap. I lived in jeans and running shoes, and the circles under my eyes disappeared.

I ate an early supper to get out of the house before Betsy started her cocktail hour and before Rosanne flopped herself on the couch, glued to the VCR, and gorged herself with Sara Lee cake.

I headed for town, to a 12-Step meeting and to join some fellow sober people for tea and desert.

By ten-thirty, I drove back out to 'Sconset, walk the dogs and went to bed, feeling safe without having a loaded gun in my night table. It was also comforting to have George sleep under the covers with me. After sleeping alone for so many years, I loved the warmth of his little body curled up next to me.

Dad and Dorothy arrived in 'Sconset in July. Since their marriage, Harrison had substantially cut back on his drinking. He was no longer drinking a fifth of rum a day or drinking at ten in the morning. For one thing, Dorothy prepared his meals so he wasn't drinking on an empty stomach. But, on occasion, he could still go into full tilt. On the nights he went over the edge, we could hear Dorothy's high shrill voice yelling, "Harrison, stop being so obnoxious."

After having lived in an alcohol-free house for five years, where it was peaceful and orderly, it was a jolt to live in the midst of this chaos. The alcoholism was so evident: Nobody listened, nobody could hear, the conversation was just like a Pinter play: everyone speaking simultaneously on different subjects at loud decibels on different frequencies.

On top of that, Betsy and Rosanne were slobs, just

like their mother. The kitchen, the bathroom, their rooms were pretty much always a mess. Every night, I ended up cleaning the mess in the kitchen and tried to keep the bathroom clean.

After Labor Day, I had another loss. My sweet little Patty, now thirteen, had become incontinent. She regularly woke up in a puddle of urine and her hind-quarter hair started to fall out because of hot spots that the urine caused.

Early in September, I drove Patty to the MSPCA in town. I took a long walk with her along the road and pine trees for our final walk. When I took her into the vet's exam room and lifted her to the table, I started to cry. The vet got the needle ready, and I said, "Oh, dearest Patty, this is the last shot you'll ever have to have."

While the vet gave her the shot, I kept my hand around her head and one hand on a front paw. Within 30 seconds, she was lifeless. I didn't have the money to have her cremated, so I left with her little green collar and matching lead.

When I got back to Sandpiper, Rosanne asked me where'd I'd been.

"I put Patty to sleep," I said, and started to cry.

Again, she never offered a condolence or kind word. She just stood there, unresponsive.

I called Maggie and George, took them into my room, and closed the door. I pulled George into bed with me and as cried, I vowed I would not spend another summer in this house.

September is a beautiful month on island, after all the summer people and tourists leave. The pace is much slower, island residents get caught up with each other, and it's still warm enough to go to the beach and swim.

Dad and Dorothy left for Key Biscayne, Rosanne left for an ashram in western Massachusetts, and Betsy and I remained in Sandpiper. It was wonderfully quiet, and I started to plan my move over to Scoop's Coop for the winter.

The first time I went into the house, I was knocked over by the odor. The bedroom had a stinky, oily smell, the bathroom had a mildew odor, and the living room and dining area also smelled awful. The stink propelled me to strip the place clean. If nothing else this summer, I'd learned how to clean houses, and this was a mission.

I emptied every drawer, closet and shelf, including linens, cutlery, glasses, liquor bottles, dishes and ugly-looking objects and boxed and stored everything in the garage. I then ordered a new box spring and mattress as well as flannel sheets and a comforter. While I was awaiting the delivery, I washed all the curtains, scrubbed every surface with bleach and water, including drawers, which I then lined with a Crabtree & Evelyn lavender-scented paper. I moved my boxes from the garage and unpacked my china, flatware and kitchen things. When the new bedding arrived, I put the bedroom together and brought over all my little things from Sandpiper and had my telephone line put into Scoop's Coop. Next was setting up my computer in the living room and putting away my summer clothes.

Finally, it was all clean, and I did my sage ceremony to chase away all the traces of alcohol.

After living in Miami for nine years, I had no winter clothes. So I went to the Nantucket Thrift Shop, where I bought five pairs of corduroy pants, at fifty cents a pair, five sweaters at two dollars apiece and a down coat, a Valentino, for fifteen dollars. For a total of twenty-seven dollars and fifty cents, I had a winter wardrobe. The only thing left to get was a job.

I applied to the Nantucket Beacon and was hired as a part-time reporter, starting after Columbus Day. It paid less than cleaning, but I was back doing what I loved to do: writing.

Two weeks later, a ferocious nor'easter hit Nantucket, and the police came down to Codfish Park to evacuate everyone. It was called a "hundred-year storm" because a storm of this intensity hits only once in a century. Betsy and I filled a laundry basket with clean clothes and food, put it in the back of my car with the three dogs and drove to a bluff house owned by one of her clients. Thank goodness the house had lots of candles, matches and a gas stove. The power was out, so we lighted the candles and put our things in the two back bedrooms.

I put Maggie and George in the bedroom where I was staying, and Betsy put Blue in her bedroom. The house was luxurious, and even though we were in the maids' quarters, each bedroom had its own bath with a tub. We luxuriated in our respective tubs, then headed to the kitchen some hot soup, forced the dogs out for a quick pee and toweled them dry before retiring for the night.

At seven o'clock the next morning, we drove back down to Codfish Park to survey the damage. We were shocked to see that the front porch was gone, half of Rosanne's bedroom was hanging over the beach with a direct drop of twenty feet to high tide, and all the property between the house and the ocean was gone.

"Oh, my God, Betsy, we're going to have to move Sandpiper or lose the house in the next storm," I said.

Ernest Gray Smith, my paternal grandfather, a newspaper pubisher, historian and world traveler.

Margorie Harvey Smith, my paternal grandmother, an artist, a civic leader and world traveler. Granny always traveled abroad with her easel and paints; here she is in Positano, Italy, in 1954.

*Joan Christopher Smith,
my mother and my
father's first wife.*

*Harrison Harvey Smith,
my father, holding me as
a 1-year-old, in 1943, in
Bear Creek, Pennsylvania.*

My sisters Susan, left, and Marjorie flank me, Christmas 1947, at Granny's house.

Christmas day at Granny's, 1947. It was the family custom for everyone to put on a costume from Granny's dress-up box. Back row: Aunt Jo, my grandmother's sister; her son, Ben Torrey; my father, Harrison; Granny; Aunt Lois, my father's sister; Uncle DeWitt; his wife, Bobbi. Front: Peggy, Dad's second wife, holding Susan; me; Marjorie.

Barbara DeWitt Smith, the adolescent years, 1957.

My senior graduation photo, 1959.

A young career woman, living in New York City, 1962.

My blond years, working as a model in Madrid, Spain, 1964.

Sipping champagne on the Queen Mary, 1966, New York City.

My wedding day, at the Plaza Hotel, December 1966, with my husband, Burt Eskow.

My wedding day, December 1971, to Peter Rient at the Cosmopolitan Club in New York.

The Smith sisters, Christmas Day, 1984, visiting our father, the merry widower, at his Key Biscayne, home from left, Marjorie, Rosanne, Susan, Betsy, and me.

Dad at his cabin in Pennsylvania with my two dogs, Buffy and Patty, 1985.

*Horse-trekking on the west coast of Ireland, across the
Connemara trail, May 1988.*

My beloved dogs: a) Smudge, the poodle, and Sure Shot, the English springer spaniel, 1970, New York; b) from left, Buffy, Patty, George, and Maggie, in Coconut Grove, Fla., 1990; c) springer spaniel Tess in Connecticut, 1997; d) springer spaniel Tracy, in Ojai, Calif., 2007; e) Wheaten terrier Charlie in Los Angeles, 2011.

Dad and his third wife, Dorothy, Key Biscayne, 1991. He was so happy with Dorothy.

The Smith sisters Barbara, Marjorie, Rosanne, and Betsy standing behind Dad for his 94th birthday celebration on Nantucket, 2009.

Our happy household in Los Angeles, Fred Miller and I with the cat, Curious, and Charlie, our Wheaten terrier, December 2013.

14 *Fall 1991–1992*

Two days later, Betsy packed her car, took Blue and left Nantucket for the winter. Despite the storm's damage to Sandpiper, I felt safe in Scoop's Coop since it was a good fifty feet back from the edge of the deck. There was no more dune in front; also gone were the dune grass, snow fence and gentle slope of the beach.

I was not only busy settling into my new quarters and a new job, I had a new friend. A woman had just moved into a cottage around the corner.

That first winter was tough. It was cold, and the wind never stopped blowing. I was so glad for my down coat and my new friend, Sondra. She was a newcomer, too, just moved from New York, so we were both getting used to the Nantucket winter. We visited for hours for tea, dinners and walking the dogs along the bluff.

Getting used to Scoop's Coop was an adjustment. The cottage didn't have any storm windows, which made heating the living room and dining room a joke. Although the house was winterized, the baseboard heat created astronomical electric bills.

Thankfully, each room had its own thermostat. So I kept the living room and dining room set at fifty-five degrees and the bedroom at sixty-five when I was gone. The bathroom heater was a godsend. Basically, I was confined to the bedroom and bathroom. When I left the house, it was too cold for George and Maggie to come out of the bedroom.

My first winter electric bill was a jolt: three hundred

dollars. I panicked because I was only netting a hundred and fifty dollars a week. As it was, I was being very frugal and managing to live on six hundred dollars a month, which paid for my food, dog food, gas and my phone bill. But the newspaper was closing for two weeks over the Christmas holiday, which meant only three hundred dollars to live on for a whole month.

I couldn't afford to pay my heating bill, and I wasn't going to have enough money for food for December and January.

I didn't want to ask my father for money; I was still upset about how we'd parted in September. When I drove Dorothy and him to the airport, Dad got out of the car and walked straight into the terminal without a thank-you, a hug or a goodbye. At least Dorothy had the heart to say thank you and goodbye. It let me see what Cynde had been telling me for years. "Going to your father is like going to an empty well."

I had no choice but to seek public assistance. I swallowed my pride and went to the social services office in Nantucket a few days before Christmas and applied for food stamps and fuel assistance. I felt so ashamed about not having any money, but the administrator was kind and understanding. I filled out the papers she gave me and handed them back to her.

"Here, dear. I know it's difficult. Here's a coupon for a free turkey at the A&P, so you'll have a turkey for Christmas, and here are food coupons for the rest of the trimmings," she said, handing them to me.

I took the coupons with a mixture of relief and dejection.

That afternoon I went to the post office, where I had a package from Dorothy. Even though it was two days before Christmas, I decided to open it anyway. I desperately needed some cheering up.

When I opened the box—a plain white one, not from a store—there were three unwrapped items: a pair of cheap black gloves that bore a tag, "Genuine leather;" a sample bottle of perfume with a label that read "Channel No. 5" (no, that is not a typo); and a non-apparel item that is still a mystery.

My first reaction was astonishment. This was my Christmas gift? From my father? And then I got angry.

"I'm not accepting any more goddam crumbs," I said out loud, and I immediately got some stationery and wrote a note:

"Dear Dorothy, I know it's the thought that counts. And so I thank you for the thought. But the gloves are not my size and since they are unlined, they're not useful here on Nantucket. And the perfume is not the fragrance I use. So I am returning them to you. If you want to get me something that I need or want, enclosed is an order form from L.L. Bean for two pairs of long underwear. Happy holidays. Love, Barbara."

I wrapped the box and drove right back up to the post office to mail it.

No more crumbs. Man, it felt good to say that out loud to myself.

Even though I was cash poor, I had ordered modest gifts from Tiffany's for them. Getting this bottom-of-the-barrel junk reminded me of when my father used to get Christmas gifts for my sisters at unclaimed freight in Wilkes-Barre. One year, he gave Rosanne a boy's bicycle from there. I'll say one thing about Peggy, she never bought a cheap gift.

On my way out of the post office, I ran into Carol Benchley, a longtime family friend. She'd been Betsy's roommate at boarding school, and Betsy had introduced Carol to her husband, Rob Benchley.

"Hi, Barbara, how are you?" Carol asked.

When I told her about the gifts that I'd just mailed back, she laughed.

"Somehow I'm not surprised. Dorothy sent us a wedding gift of four black hand towels from J.C. Penney," she said.

"You're joking," I said. "It just shows she doesn't know any better. You know how fond Dad is of you and Rob. Even he'd be embarrassed about the towels."

On May first, I got a call from my father saying that he and Dorothy were arriving on island on May fifteenth. They had originally planned to arrive mid-June.

"But, Dad, where are you staying?" I asked.

"Well, in the cottage, of course," he answered testily.

"But there's only one bedroom. That means there will be the three of us with the two dogs," I said, and I could hear the anxiety in my voice.

"Yes?" he responded. "So?"

Good god. The cottage was free of alcohol and chaos, and now it was going to be invaded. I no longer had eight weeks to get the cottage ready, just two. And it was going to be a scramble to find new living quarters for myself as well as putting all their stuff back.

Cynde once told me that every trauma I'd experienced in my past was something I would have to re-experience in sobriety so that I could make closure on it, to keep my past from recurring. Little comfort that was right now.

That Sunday I took a stroll after church to think about what to do, and walking along Low Beach Road with Maggie and George, I saw a little cottage set back from the road. On an impulse, I walked into the driveway.

"Are you looking for something?"

I looked over in the direction of the voice and saw a

woman in the neighboring yard speaking to me. I walked over and introduced myself.

"Do you know if this cottage is available?" I asked.

"Funny you should ask," she said. "It just came on the market an hour ago. The two people who had rented it for the summer arrived this morning and said it was too small, and they cancelled their lease. The owner just went into town to the real estate agent."

I got the name of the owner and left a note for her. She called later that afternoon, and I drove back down with the dogs to meet her.

As I drove into the shell driveway, a nice-looking woman came out of the main house, about fifty feet from the little cottage. We introduced ourselves and shook hands, and then she showed me the place.

It was a studio cottage with unpainted planking, and the patina gave it the feel of a cabin. There were two lofts, one on each side. And in the front corner was a desk with a chair behind it. I went over and sat in it, and looked out of the window and heard the voice in my head say: This is where you are going to write the book.

With that, I looked up at the owner and said, "I want to take it for the summer. How much is it?"

"Well, we were asking six thousand dollars for it, but since there's no agent's commission, how about five thousand?"

"Could I have it until October 15?" I asked.

"Yes, that's not a problem," she replied.

"And could I move in immediately?"

"Yes, that would be fine. We've never had dogs before," she said hesitantly.

I had the feeling that she liked me, and that I looked like a dependable tenant, a bird in the hand, so to speak.

"The dogs are very well-behaved and they've got references if you'd like. Come on out to the car and meet them for yourself," I said.

We walked to my car, and I let the dogs out onto the driveway, where Maggie and George did their adorable dog act. They sat on command and looked well-behaved.

"And not to worry," I assured her. "I pick up after them, so there'll be no droppings in the yard. I'd love to move in, and frankly, the only problem is, I've got to get some money. I'll get back to you in two days at the most," I promised.

I drove back to Codfish Park, and made a call to a Miami friend. All I got was his answering machine, so I left my name and number and asked if he could please get back to me as soon as possible

That night, my friend returned my call.

"Hi, DeWitt. It's David. I just got back from a long weekend, and in two days, I'm leaving Miami for a month. It's a good thing you called now. Otherwise, you wouldn't have been able to reach me."

When I told him my predicament and asked if he'd be able to lend me the rent, he said, "I'll be glad to lend you the money. Why don't I round it off to six thousand dollars so you have a little extra? I'll put a check in the mail tomorrow morning."

I thanked him profusely, and when I hung up, I got down on my knees and said a prayer. Man, this was proof I had a guardian angel.

The next morning I went back down to Low Beach Road to the cottage and found the owner in her front yard.

"Hi, Lois," I waved, and walked over to her. "I've got the money. It's arriving later this week, and I'll give you the whole amount in one check. But I have a tremendous favor to ask. May I move in tomorrow afternoon?"

"Of course, you can," she said. "I'm so happy for both of us."

"Thanks so much, Lois, for letting move in before the check arrives. It helps me out so much."

The next day, a colleague from the Beacon who had a moving trailer helped me pack up and move. I worked feverishly the rest of the day to set up my new nest. I'd been lucky about getting hold of the telephone company to get my phone disconnected at Scoop's Coop and transfer the number to the new cottage.

Once I'd gotten everything in place, the only thing left was to figure out where George was going to sleep. He'd been sharing my bed for five years, and when I climbed the ladder that night to the loft, he sat at the bottom whimpering. Maggie climbed onto the love seat, which became her bed for the rest of the summer. I couldn't stand George's crying, so I climbed down, lifted him in my arms and carried him up to the loft, where he curled up next to me under the covers and on the flannel sheets. That was our sleeping arrangement for the rest of the summer. The loft had a double mattress, under a skylight. So I was able to watch the stars until I fell asleep.

The next morning was a sunny, beautiful June day, the start of a new routine. The shower was outside, at the back of the cottage in a circular wooden enclosure. As I stood under the hot water, I looked over the top of the fence to see a hundred acres of wild flowers. I made my breakfast, walked the dogs, and called Betsy.

"Betsy, I've moved," and explained the whole thing. "Will you be willing to give me the houses I had last year for cleaning?"

"You bet. I'm so glad for you, Ba. I hadn't made up a schedule for the houses yet," she said.

All that remained was cleaning Scoop's Coop and putting the stored stuff in the garage back before Dad and Dorothy arrived.

I put everything back in place, and two weeks later, I drove into town to join some pals for lunch. They were waiting for me inside in line, and a man who'd been talking with them, turned to me and said, "I hope you're joining us for lunch. My name is Kent."

15 *1993–1994*

A DEPRESSION SETTLED in on me after Sandpiper washed away. Even though I was safely tucked away in my cousins' house, the only relief I had from the depression was the dream workshop in Connecticut and going to New York twice to see Kent.

Those two weekends were full of passion, good meals and laughs. But he called the following week and said his wife had found out about us. He ended the call by saying he wanted no communication for six weeks while he "evaluated his marriage."

During those six weeks, I felt utterly deserted. One night when I was crying myself to sleep, again, I had a flash.

"Oh, my God, this is the abandonment I felt when my mother left. This is the deep, deep pain I've been running from all these years."

That poor little four-year-old who didn't know where her mother had gone, and was told I was never going to see my mother again. No one had told me anything except that I wasn't allowed to mention her. This is why I felt like an emotional orphan. My mother was gone, my father was absent, there was no one to love me, to hold me, to protect me or tell me what was going on.

When I shared this with Sondra the next day, she said: "This brings up all the neglect. It's recalling all the neglect you suffered. I've heard you speak of your father's mother. What about your mother's mother?"

"I never knew her. Neither did my mother, for that matter. She died in childbirth," I replied.

"So your mother did to you what was done to her," she said quietly.

Her remark was an insight into how family history repeats itself.

"My mother once told me that the reason she left my father was because of his drinking. My father thinks she left him for another man. But the fact is, she left him for a man who didn't drink. She told me that my father drank, he got crazy and she just couldn't stand it," I said

"She left in order to take care of herself. That took a lot of courage," she said.

Six weeks later, Kent called.

"Hi, sweetheart. How are you?" he purred.

I was breathless, awaiting his verdict.

"What did you decide, darling?"

"I decided that I want you in my life," he answered.

My heart skipped a beat.

"You mean you're going to leave your wife?" I asked.

"No. I decided I want you in my life," he repeated.

"I don't get it, Kent. What are you telling me?"

"I can't leave her. I just can't do it. I can't stand to see her pain. But I want you in my life," he said.

It took a moment for me to get the message. He wanted his cake and to eat it, too. Zeus wanted to keep Hera at home, despite their maintaining separate bedrooms and having a passionless marriage. But he also didn't want to give up Aphrodite. He wanted to get laid.

"You tell me you love me and that you don't want to be without me. Please, Kent, tell me what's really going on."

"It's not about leaving my wife. It's about leaving my life," he said. "I just can't do it."

And then he hung up.

When I got up the next morning, a surging rage replaced the tears. I was so goddam mad at Kent, so goddam mad about being neglected and deserted. I remembered the anger work at Caron and decided to do some on my own. Right after breakfast I drove into town to Marine Lumber, bought an ax and drove back to 'Sconset. I got out of the car and headed for the front porch where I got a couple of logs, set them up in the yard and started splitting wood. Every time I brought the blade down against the wood, I screamed from my gut. Swinging the ax was a lot more strenuous than swinging the bataka bat and, after ten minutes, my throat and arms were tired. But I felt a whole lot better.

I called Sondra to tell her about my ax therapy.

"That's great. I'm glad you're doing something to get rid of the anger instead of letting it eat you up," she said.

That spring when I moved out of my cousins' house and back to the little cottage on Low Beach Road, I had to re-organize my life. The reason for coming to Nantucket was to live rent free while I wrote the book. But that plan had been literally blown out of the water.

I didn't want to see my father and Dorothy that summer. I just couldn't bear the thought of visiting the new house, "Dorothy's house" as my sisters and I called it.

When I got my share of the insurance check for the

property loss, I called a friend in Palm Beach and mentioned casually that I was thinking about moving to New York.

"When?" she asked.

"About October fifteenth. That's when my lease runs out here."

"I've got the perfect apartment for you. Babette's co-op is available on October first."

Babette was her daughter.

"Is there any problem about dogs? I've got two, you know."

"I don't think so. I've seen other dogs in the building," she said, and she told me about the apartment and where it was.

She gave me Babette's phone number, and I called right away. We hadn't seen each other in ten years, not since we both lived on Key Biscayne, when her mother and my father had dated. Later that month, Babette called to say she'd gotten very sick and couldn't move. Instead, she gave me the number of another owner in her building who wanted a tenant. I called him, and made a deal to move in October 15. I was feeling a lot more secure now that I had a place to live.

I still wondered about the meaning of the dream. What did Rome mean? And what did midnight mean?

The answer came to me during one of my nightly walks in 'Sconset with the dogs. I flashed back to seeing my father in the living room in Shrine View while he read "The Rise and Decline of the Roman Empire." But the phrase in my head said, "The Rise and Decline of the Roman Emperor, The Rise and Decline of the Roman Emperor."

The clue came from Robbie's question about a homophone: Is it R-O-M-E or R-O-A-M? It wasn't Empire. It was Emperor. I had to get to Rome—the seat of the emperor—before midnight. I had to get to Rome before the emperor died. I had to make peace with my father before he died.

That's what the dream meant! My subconscious was telling me to make peace with my father before he died, before it was too late.

The next day I called my father.

"Hi, Dad. It's Barbara."

"Well, Barbara, it's so good to hear from you," he said.

We made a lunch date for later that week, and when we met, he allowed me to hug him instead of pulling away, as he usually did.

During lunch, I told him about my plans to move to New York, and that I'd gotten the apartment through our old friend, Babette.

He was pleased for me and invited me to a farewell party he and Dorothy were having. I accepted, and I felt good to see them happy in their new house.

Six days later I moved into the penthouse with my two dogs and my new possessions from the Nantucket Auction.

I hadn't lived in Manhattan for fifteen years. After living in the quiet and clean air of Wilkes-Barre, Miami and Nantucket, it took some getting used to. It was no more opening the door to let the dogs out. Walking the dogs meant leashes and finding a route to Central Park.

I spent the rest of the month setting up camp and getting my new home in order. I also got in touch with old friends who still lived in the city.

At Christmas time, a dear friend from Washington

came for a two-day visit. We hadn't seen each other for seven years and catching up was a treat. She gave me two books, "The Gods in Everyman," and "The Goddesses in Everywoman."

"It's written by a Jungian psychologist, and they're wonderful," Lorraine said.

That night, I couldn't put the books down and reading them made me want to get back into therapy.

"My dreams have been so vivid and lucid over the past couple of years that I've kept a notebook."

"Listen, D.W."—that was her nickname for me—"there are no accidents. It just so happens I know a Jungian therapist here in New York. We've been friends for years. Let me give you his name and number, and let me know what happens."

After Lorraine left, I called the therapist, and we made an appointment for the following week.

The therapy with Steve was different from working with Cynde. By being in group therapy with her, I'd seen how she worked before I started seeing her individually. I trusted her, and she knew my history.

Steve and I were starting anew. I started with my personal history—the names of the family members, how old I was at the time of the particular events in my life, my experience with my own alcoholism, how and when I'd stopped drinking, the start of my recovery and my previous therapy. I also told him that I'd been keeping a dream journal for four years and that I'd like to explore those dreams with him.

"Tell me about your marriages. You said you've been divorced twice," Steve said.

"My first marriage was to a man who was ten years older than I was. He protected me from Peggy. Once I was married, she couldn't get at me anymore. But the marriage lasted just eighteen months. He was so highly critical, and I couldn't stand it any longer."

"So your marriage was a way to escape your family," Steve said quietly.

I'd never thought of it that way, but it was the truth.

"What about the second marriage?" he asked.

I told him the saga about Edward and Peter, and how I'd left Edward, who offered me everything that I'd ever wanted for a stable life, and went off with Peter, the alcoholic. I'd left the loving kind man for the bad boy, the one who slept with is best friend's fiancée. And I left Peter because of his alcoholism.

"I'm also here because I'm in a bad relationship, and I want to end it. I want to break my pattern of having unavailable men in my life."

A week later, I had my second session, which finished my history. The third session was the day of my birthday. I love my birthday, and have ever since I was a little girl. I always awoke with a sense of excitement and promise. This morning was no different.

Later that morning I went downtown a tai chi class, then met a friend for lunch, did some reading, walked Maggie and George and went to Steve's for my appointment. Although I'd started the day light-hearted, by five o'clock, the time of my appointment, there was something gnawing at me. I sat down and told him that it was my birthday and how I'd spent it.

"But I'm feeling a little sad now," I said.

"What's going on with you?"

"I haven't heard from Kent in two weeks, not since I saw him."

Despite my resolve to break it off with Kent, I'd broken down and contacted him. The loneliness was too overwhelming. We saw each other, and he promised he'd call in a day or two.

"How do you feel about that?" Steve asked.

"I'm really upset about it. I feel so frustrated again, because I can't call him to find out what's going on. It's just like last year when he cancelled our plans for my birthday dinner. And it's just like it was when I was growing up. I never had a birthday with my father and Peggy. They always went to a two-day newspaper convention in Philadelphia that fell on the same date as my birthday. I don't ever remember getting a birthday present from them, just souvenirs from the convention," I said. I could feel the tears start to well up in my throat.

"Souvenirs from a convention were your birthday present?" Steve asked.

When I heard his tone of voice, it dawned on me that Peggy and Dad never considered getting a present for me. They were two alcoholics too busy with their social schedule.

Tears ran down my cheeks. I was silent some more and then pulled out my dream notebook.

"I had a dream the other night that I can't decipher. I'd like to read it to you.

"I'm in a life boat. There's one other person, a faceless man. All of a sudden we're going over a towering waterfall. I lean back to brace myself. I get the paddle out of the way, and even though I'm afraid, I'm not terrified. I keep my eyes open as it plunges toward the bottom. That's the end of the dream."

"Well, it sounds to me like you're getting your eyes back and that you're willing to keep them open," Steve said quietly.

I took that in, and thought about how often I'd gone through my life with my eyes closed. How many times had I seen danger and ignored it, just closed my eyes? I did that with Peter. The day before our wedding, a friend asked if I had any misgivings about the marriage.

"Yes, I'm concerned that Peter drinks too much," I said.

But my reservation didn't stop me from going through with the wedding. If I'd been paying attention—had my eyes open—I wouldn't have married him. If I'd had my eyes open, I wouldn't have left Edward.

I've paid a high price for keeping my eyes closed, for ignoring reality and being in denial. That's why I was back in therapy.

As I continued to work with Steve, I told him about the book. He asked why I was writing it.

"I want to show that emotional healing is possible. And I want to expose all the insanity and lies that lurk behind the looking-good family, to show that money and privilege don't protect children from abuse or from neglect," I said.

When I got back to the apartment, there was a message from Kent. He was calling from Florida, where he was on his annual winter trip with his wife. It was another reality check about his being married. I needed to keep my eyes open.

I was running low on money and found a job as a copy editor at a legal publishing company. I loved being back in an office, which was a comfortable one. Because I was a part-time employee, I could set my own hours. So I worked from ten to six, except on Fridays when I left at four-thirty for my appointment with Steve. All the copy editors had their own cubicles, with a desk and computer and style book. I put up my Nantucket calendar, some photos and some dried flowers to make it cozy for eight hours a day.

Best of all, the work was interesting. Each morning, I went into the copy chief's office to pick up a stack of pages.

The stacks were page proofs to be checked and corrected before being sent to the printer, and the copy editors were the last eyes to see the work. Sometimes it was a chapter, sometimes it was a couple of chapters being updated. Because federal and state laws were constantly being revised and new opinions written and new court decisions being handed down, there was a steady stream of updating for these legal reference books. That spring I read a lot about aviation law and environmental law. One morning I picked up a stack with the title, "The Child As a Client."

I started reading the copy as an editor, and the material covered case law and procedures for dealing with abused children who had to be removed from their natural or foster homes. My reading slowed down when I got to the chapter on the "failure-to-thrive syndrome."

A particular description really caught my attention.

"The failure-to-thrive syndrome can be seen in children who suffer extreme physical developmental lags, such as being underweight; children who are chronically hungry; children who are chronically tired."

It also described the syndrome's emotional component: Children who lack emotional nourishment simply fail to grow. And those who are attacked, threatened or intimidated have increased levels of depression, anger and anxiety.

I closed the folder for a minute and took a deep breath. So this explained why I was ten pounds underweight a child; this was why I felt listless and tired and slept in the school rest room off the library; the hunger was a symptom of neglect. I wasn't being fed regularly. It also explained my suicidal thoughts from time to time: no one loved me enough to take care of me properly.

I was being educated about the state of my childhood and learned that it had a legal name. After my mother left, I spent the rest of my childhood and teen-age years never being hugged, kissed or being told, "I love you." I grew up with an absence of love and no emotional nourishment, in other words, emotional impoverishment.

On my way to Steve's that week, I saw a woman and a little boy waiting at a corner. A city bus stopped, and I saw them watch the exiting passengers. The child's face lit up when he spotted a man stepping off the bus, and the man picked up the little boy and lifted him to his shoulder for a big hug. It was something I'd never experienced with my father.

No wonder the tie to Kent was so strong. He was the only one who hugged and kissed me and told me that he loved me. And if he went away, I'd have no one. I'd be left with that awful longing to be loved.

For the rest of the summer, Steve and I worked on that point. By fall, he shared three important points with me. The first had to do with the molestation.

"You were initiated into sex much earlier than most females are."

The word "initiated" gave me a new understanding about what had happened. The phrase "being initiated" also removed the sense of being victimized.

The second thing that Steve said: "Moms come and go in your household, but your father always stays. He's always there." He held his gaze as he said that. And I saw that although my father wasn't always responsive in the way I wanted him to be, he was, in fact, always there in person and financially and that he loved me in his own way.

The most powerful thing Steve told me was: "When you can invite a kind, loving, considerate man into your life, you will have broken with your family history."

16 *1994–1995*

BY THE END of my lease, I couldn't afford to live in New York any longer and found a place about thirty miles north of the city. The movers loaded all my things into the truck, and the dogs and I sat on the front seat for the forty-five mile ride to Nyack.

My routine changed drastically. First, I became a commuter. Getting to the office used to take me twenty minutes; now it took an hour and a half. I left at eight a.m. and returned at seven p.m. Living in the suburbs also meant I needed a car; I bought a friend's old Ford station wagon for five hundred dollars.

Despite the commute, living in Nyack was pleasant. It was quiet, and I no longer had to dodge traffic when I walked the dogs.

Once I'd gotten my apartment all settled, including hanging the paintings, mostly done by my grandmother, I noticed that all of them were landscapes or houses. It got me thinking about how much I wanted to settle down. But because of the continually shrinking newspaper business, I had had to keep moving to find work.

That evening, just for the hell of it, I made a list of how many times I'd moved since I'd left Shrine View. I knew it was a lot, but the actual count startled me.

"Fifty-five moves in thirty-five years?" I re-counted. "That's nuts."

A lot of the moves were in the same city, primarily New York, because I was reluctant to rent a place for a year. I kept hoping I'd meet a man who would sweep me into his arms, his life and his apartment. That's why I never bought any furniture or established a home of my own. I was always doing six-month sublets of somebody else's furnished home. I was like a waif going from shelter to shelter.

I went to bed early on New Year's Eve and was excited about the next day. Kent said he could spend the afternoon with me.

He was due at one. At a quarter to one, he called.

"I'm sorry, baby. I can't come. Some neighbors just came by the house, and I've got to stay. I gotta go. I'll call you next week," he said hastily and hung up.

That was it? I was fucking furious. And for the first time, the fury made me see that *I* was the fool for staying in a relationship with a married man. *I* was the one doing the same thing over and over again expecting different results. *I* was the one who was tolerating continued bad behavior. What a dope *I'd* been.

That night Kent called and suggested we meet next Saturday.

"We can exchange our Christmas gifts, sweetheart, and I'll make it up to you," he said in his seductive voice.

"Okay, darling. I'll see you next Saturday," I said, knowing that my agenda was a kiss-off scene, after today's stunt.

The following Saturday, I was all ready at one o'clock. He showed up at two.

"Oh, baby, it's so good to see you," he said.

I took his coat and said, "Sit down, sweetheart. I want to give you my Christmas gift."

We exchanged gifts, and when he thanked me for his, I spoke clearly and without any emotion.

"Kent, I'm calling it off. Last weekend showed me that I can't ever count on you to show up, even if we have plans. I'm not putting up with it any more. I wanted to see you today to tell you in person," I said.

I saw his face go from smiling to cold.

"I think I'd better go."

And he got up and left. After two and a half years, all he could say was, "I think I'd better go."

Today I came out of denial because I had kept my eyes open.

Later that summer, my friend Gerilyn called, and we made plans for her to come out to Nyack for the weekend.

Gerilyn and I had met on Key Biscayne nine years ago when we both lived there. By the time I left for Nantucket, we'd become close friends, and she felt like a sister to me. When I moved to Nantucket, she came to visit. When I moved to New York, she moved to Brooklyn Heights a few months later. And because she had a car, it was Gerilyn who'd driven me to Nyack when I started looking to live outside the city.

In our last conversation, she said couldn't stand the noise of the city any longer, so I suggested she come take a look at Nyack.

"Gerilyn, there's a wonderful community out here. You'll have no trouble getting work, there are clean places to run, and it's peaceful and quiet and safe," I said.

She arrived on a Friday night, and we spent a couple of hours catching up. The next morning, I was in the living room when she came back from a run.

"Oh, DeWitt, it's so beautiful here. I ran along the river, and the trees and houses along this street are wonderful."

She had the local paper to check out rentals, and I gave her some pointers about where to look.

When she returned that afternoon, Gerilyn told me about all the places she'd seen. There were a bunch of messages for her on my phone, and so she returned calls and made appointments for the next day. Later, when we sat down for dinner, she told me she'd been in a rocky mental place and was feeling suicidal.

"Gerilyn, I was there, too. Remember? You saw me when I was unraveling in Miami. What helped me was seeing Cynde and going to Caron."

I also reminded her about the Buddhist belief of reincarnation and the karma of interrupting our lives.

"I just don't believe that anymore. That's a lot of dogma a lot of old men in robes are shoving down our throats. I just don't believe in anything any more," she said with a very flat affect.

"1 know how much you'll love this community. Once you move out here, you'll have a change of heart," I said.

"Well, last night was the first good sleep I've had in weeks. It's so quiet and so peaceful. You know how noise affects me, and with this heat, the city's unbearable," she said.

I gave her a hug and went to bed. The next day, we did the same routine. When she got back from running, she checked out the Sunday paper, made her calls and left.

When she got back, she said, "I found a place and put a deposit down."

It was the first time I'd heard some life in her voice and a tone of excitement since she'd arrived. She told me about the apartment, which was only two blocks away from me. "We'll be neighbors in two weeks."

I was so happy for both of us. Finally I was going to have a good friend here in Nyack. After supper, I gave her the name of my mover. At the end of the evening, we hugged and she left for the city.

On Thursday, I got a postcard from her, an Edward Hopper reproduction from the Whitney Museum, where she'd been to see the Hopper exhibit. The connection was that Hopper had lived in Nyack, and she made reference to that. I put the card on my desk.

The next night, Friday, the phone rang just after eleven.

"Hello?"

"Is this DeWitt?" a woman's voice asked.

"Yes, it is."

"This is Gerilyn's cousin, Stevie, and I'm calling to say the police have found a body in Gerilyn's apartment," and the woman started to cry.

I knew of Stevie because Gerilyn had spoken of her so often.

She collected herself and continued.

"Gerilyn's brother called the police after he'd been unable to reach her for several days. When the police got there, the landlord had to let them in. That's when they'd discovered a body of a woman who had died of a gunshot wound to the head," Stevie sobbed.

She explained that the police retrieved Gerilyn's address book and gave it to her brother. The brother then gave the address book to Stevie, which is how she got my name and number.

Even though we'd never met, we'd both heard about each other, and Stevie knew that Gerilyn had spent last weekend with me.

The news left me in a state of shock.

"Stevie, I don't understand. Are you sure it's Gerilyn? She was supposed to go to a Buddhist retreat this weekend, and she'd just signed a lease for an apartment here in Nyack," I said.

Her voice broke again. She said there'd be no way of knowing for sure until the brother returned from the morgue.

"I just needed to talk with someone who loved her as much as I did, DeWitt. I have a terrible feeling about this."

"Yes, so do I, Stevie. Please call me as soon as you know, no matter what time," I said.

I went to bed and started to cry. I knew deep down that Gerilyn was dead and had killed herself. Last weekend she told me she'd bought a gun. I couldn't stop crying because the grief was so deep. At six-thirty that morning, the phone rang. I knew it was Stevie.

"DeWitt, it's Stevie. It was her. Even though the body was badly decomposed, the medical examiner identified her," she said, crying.

"I know, I know. I've been crying all night, Stevie. I can't seem to stop. I don't have any more energy to talk right now. Thank you so much for letting me know. I'll call you later in the day," I said.

I went over to the desk where the postcard was. It had been mailed Wednesday. So she'd been alive then. I looked at her handwriting and started to cry again.

"Gerilyn, if you'd only hung on. If you'd only called me," I said out loud.

For the next several days, I couldn't stop thinking, "If only she'd called."

Her suicide reminded me of that day in Coconut Grove when I was on my way out the door to buy a thirty-eight, the same type of gun that Gerilyn had bought and used. But the moment I crossed the doorway to go buy the gun, my phone rang. Now I saw how that telephone call had pulled me back from that moment of desperation.

17 *Fall 1995*

A MONTH AFTER Gerilyn's death, I called Cynde and asked about the day I'd been suicidal seven years ago.

"Cynde, about a year after I got back from Caron, I remember your saying that you said you weren't sure I was going to make it that day. What did you mean?"

"You were in a precarious place, and I said that based on the facts as they existed. It was more of an intuitive response," she said. "You were also in such pain, you were looking for a quick way out."

I told her how Gerilyn's death had affected me. I also talked about my history with Kent and that I was exhausted from what seemed to be "the long goodbye." I told her about the last goodbye.

"You're retraumatizing yourself every time you say goodbye. That's what it was like with your mother when she visited you because you never knew when you were going to see her again," she explained.

I absorbed Cynde's words and understood another piece of the puzzle: I'd been re-creating the drama of my childhood without knowing it. It was true. I never knew when Kent was going to call. One time it was a year between phone calls. It pointed up my core issue: abandonment. I thanked her for her insight, and we said goodbye.

October arrived, time for my father's eightieth birthday. He was hosting a dinner-dance in Wilkes-Barre for all his friends. I thought I'd skip the whole thing, but when I told Cynde, she was amazed.

"You're not going?" she asked. "You've been excluded most of your life from your family gatherings. DeWitt, you don't need to exclude yourself now."

Oh, right. Another ah-ha moment!

I called Dad and said I'd love to be there. I also offered to be the photographer and make a birthday album for him. He was happy I was coming and made arrangements for me to stay at the North Mountain Club, a hunting and fishing club adjacent to his cabin and property.

I appreciated the offer, since I didn't want to stay at the cabin with Susan, Dorothy and him. He also mentioned that Marjorie, Rosanne and Betsy had made arrangements to stay with old school friends.

It had been fifteen years since I'd been in Wilkes-Barre, and I called an old classmate to make a lunch date. Jane said she'd round up some other classmates to join us.

The drive to Pennsylvania was beautiful. The fall had been a spectacular Indian summer, with the leaves all orange and red. It was late afternoon when I arrived at the clubhouse and the three-bedroom guest house. When I drove up, I spotted four deer grazing in the front meadow. As soon as they heard the car, they took off and cleared the stone wall and ran into the woods. I marveled at their beauty and agility.

I let the dogs out of the car and took a deep breath of the clean, cool air and took in the view. North Mountain was where Dad used to take the five of us hiking and where I acquired my love of the woods. It felt wonderful to be here. I unpacked, fed the dogs and headed back into town for dinner with the mother of a friend.

Mrs. Graham was the woman I always wanted to have for a mother. Her daughter, Jane, and I had gone to school since nursery class, and we went through the ninth grade before I went off to boarding school. Because we both lived in the country, Jane and I spent more time together that I did with other classmates. Whenever I was on a sleep-over at the Graham house, I basked in Mrs. Graham's soft-spoken kindness. Dinner at their house was uneventful, unlike Shrine View, where meals always were a battle zone.

At night, Mrs. Graham would come into Jane's bedroom and tuck us into bed and say sweetly, "Goodnight, girls."

When I arrived, Mrs. Graham looked just like she always had—an elegant looking woman who was slim and serene.

She was a widow now, living in the mother-in-law apartment the garage had been converted to. We talked about her son and granddaughter. I told her what my life had been like for the past thirty-five years, about my being a recovering alcoholic and how crazy it had been growing up in the Smith household.

"I knew there was something dreadfully wrong there, Barbara, but in those days, nobody spoke up. We were just all silent," she said. "But I remember two things. One was at the Mainwaring house. You know how what a free-wheeling house it was over there, and one night when we were all having cocktails, Connie and Hamer were running around, just as little kids do. They were probably only eight and ten, and I remember so distinctly that Peggy was talking to me and gritted her teeth and said, 'If they were mine, I'd give them the hairbrush right now.' I remember how viciously she said it."

"You know she was an alcoholic, don't you?" I asked.

"Oh, yes, she wasn't fooling anyone, although we never used that word in those days. But she could never keep her hair appointment. Never. We both had appointments at noon on Friday. And she always, always called to cancel," she said. "Of course, we all knew why," she said with a smile.

I felt a tremendous sense of relief to learn that Peggy hadn't been fooling anyone. The secrets hadn't been so secret after all.

The next day I met my friends Sally and the two Janes. I hadn't seen these women in thirty-five years. After the hugs and the "I don't believe its," we sat down and started talking as if we'd all seen each other just a week ago. I saw that childhood friendships create a bond unlike any other. Sally and I had also known each other since we'd been four years old. The other Jane and I met when we were ten. Basically, we'd known each other for half a century. We knew each other's parents, siblings, first dates, and all the information that comes from growing up together. It was heartwarming. We took turns giving brief accounts of what we'd been up to. They all were still living in the Wilkes-Barre area with their husbands and now were empty-nesters with grown children who were leading their own lives.

I told them about my marriages and divorces, being a recovering alcoholic and about the therapy I'd gone through.

"Barbara, you kids were treated like slaves out at Shrine View. Peggy had you running up and down those stairs delivering drinks and food to her bedroom. I remember how strange it was that she stayed in bed all day," Jane said. "You Smith kids had it tough. No wonder you drank. We all knew it was nuts out there."

Her remarks recalled what Cynde told me about my history. "Peggy treated you like Cinderella. She dressed you in rags and treated you like a servant."

Once again, I felt relief knowing Peggy hadn't fooled anyone.

After Sally and Jane left, the other Jane and I talked some more. I told her about my visit with her mother and asked about her impressions of Shrine View.

"I was terrified of Peggy," she said and told of how Peggy had raised her voice to her when she was there for a sleepover.

"Oh, that explains why you were there just one time and why all the other times I went to your house," I said.

"Yes," she nodded.

I was struck by her use of the word terrified.

"I spent most of my childhood terrified of Peggy," I thought.

My father had been planning his birthday party for two months. He'd sent the invitations from Nantucket and reserved the whole downstairs of the Westmoreland Club, a club where my great-grandfather was a founder, where my father had been a member for more than fifty years and I'd been a member when I'd moved back to Wilkes-Barre in 1979. I remember the first time I went there. Granny had taken me for lunch, upstairs to the ladies' dining room. I felt so grown up, especially when an old-time waiter confided to me: "Your grandmother is such a lady."

The night of the party I arrived at the club with my Nikon and twenty rolls of film, and stood by the receiving line to get shots of the arriving guests, all of whom I'd known since childhood. In addition to my sisters, there was also an array of cousins. Harrison was in fine fettle, as he always was at a party, and I'd never seen Dorothy look so pretty. They looked happy together, and I was so happy for my father and her.

The band was on a dais at the end of the dining room, with ten dinner tables around the perimeter. Cocktails were served until seven-thirty, and then dinner began. I roamed around the room and took pictures of all the tables and was so happy I hadn't exiled myself.

The after-dinner entertainment included my father singing a song in German with everyone laughing and clapping. I watched his performance and stood next to Jack Conyngham, his lifelong friend.

"He sure is having a good time, isn't he, Jack?" I said.

"He's been that way ever since he was a little boy. I've known him for seventy-five years, and he's the one who always has the best time at a party. He sure knows how to enjoy himself," Jack said.

Jack's remark prompted another "ah-ha."

"That's another legacy from him," I thought. "He taught us all how to enjoy ourselves."

When the music stopped, a family friend said, "Gee, it takes the Smiths to come back into town to get everybody out for a good time. I haven't been to a party like this in years. All we do now is go visit people in the hospital or go to funerals."

On the drive back to Nyack the next day, I thought about the evening and an ah-ha moment. It reminded me of what I'd heard Deepak Chopra say on his PBS series.

"Assaulted by insults and criticism, a child is robbed of self-worth.

The repeated absence of love and pleasure in a child creates a deep-seated and repeated yearning. Use your memories, but don't let your memories use you. If you do, you will live in a state of reaction, a victim of your past."

18 *1996–2006*

I HAD NO interest in being a victim of my past or being a member of the walking wounded. It has taken years of hard work in therapy to recalibrate my psychological bearings. I am no longer plagued by constant yearnings to be loved or feel like an emotional orphan.

This shift happened because I created a family of choice, people who were kind, trustworthy and loving.

"Tell me about your childhood friends," Cynde asked one session.

"Outside of school, I didn't really have any. We lived in the country, and there weren't any other children my age around, just my sisters," I answered.

"So what did you do?" she asked.

"I read a lot. I'd walk a couple of miles to the library and then walk back home. Books were my best friends," I said.

"They still are," Cynde said.

The truth of that made me blink hard. Whenever I wanted to hide out, I read. Once I started reading a book, no one could reach me. Sometimes I'd hole up for a couple of days. To change that habit and to start the healing process from loneliness, Cynde asked if I would be willing to put down my books, just for a while, to face my feelings.

Now I understand why it was always so heart-wrenching to leave my books behind, especially in the Coconut Grove house. It was like losing all my friends, all at once.

Therapy also taught me I didn't have to deprive myself of gifts.

Years ago, when I was in New York to meet an old friend for dinner, there was a torrential downpour an hour before we were to meet. My friend called to say he was sending a car to pick me up so I wouldn't get caught in the rain when taxis are impossible to find. When I got to the restaurant, Henry was waiting for me and greeted me warmly.

After we were seated, he asked if I wanted my usual—herbal tea and a salad. That's when I had another ah-ha moment! Here I was, in one of the best restaurants in Manhattan, with one of the most charming and powerful men in New York, what the hell was I doing having herbal tea and greens? I realized that I was doing what Peggy had done most of my life: depriving me. I vowed I'd never do that again. Depriving myself meant being stuck in my past. Tonight, I had a strong feeling of being worthwhile, that I was worthy of gifts. I smiled and answered my friend.

"No, my dear. I'd like to start with a fish course."

"Wonderful. Shall I order a little Champagne?"

"I'd love some," I said.

That was the last time I ordered tea and a salad in a three-star restaurant.

I wrote this book to share that healing from growing up in an alcoholic household is possible. The healing required working with a therapist, someone who could decode all of the secret and mixed messages embedded by alcoholic parents. Working with a therapist allowed me to have a corrective emotional experience—dissolving the emotional blocks of trauma. I was able to resolve unfinished business.

Once that happened, I no longer had any tolerance for

bad behavior and neglect. Because I had been conditioned to it, I was unable to identify bad behavior.

"Was Daddy a bad boy last night?" That was how the attraction to bad boys was planted, starting back at Shrine View. Bad boys were funny and amusing when they drank. Prince Charmings were charming but insincere. What was confusing was that Dad went to work every day. I never saw him miss a day of work or be late, and he didn't drink during the day. So it took a long time to see the "bad-boy" behavior because it was wrapped in a conventional life. Proof of my healing is I now walk away from people who behave badly. These days I have absolutely no tolerance for bad behavior.

"When you can invite a kind and loving and available man in your life, you will have broken with your family history."

Those parting words of Steve's are engraved in my psyche.

According to Scott Peck in his book, "The Road Less Traveled," children who have not received a firm commitment from their parents have a difficult time making commitments in their adult relationships.

I call it the "monkey-not-see, monkey-not-do" syndrome. I saw little or no loving behavior from my stepmother and father. What I did see was a lot of sarcasm and criticism. Peggy constantly criticized my sisters and me. "What's the matter with you? Are you stupid?" was a constant refrain.

Scott Peck's words also allowed me to see why I was so ambivalent about making a commitment to myself or to men who said they loved me.

When I was told "I love you," my internal question was "Why?"

I was incapable of understanding why anyone would love me or that I was lovable. Through therapy, I found out that until I loved myself, I would never be able to accept love from someone else.

Years later, I found surrogate parents. George and Ruth Bernard were kind, loving people, who were my landlords in West Redding, Connecticut. They always made me feel like one of the family and included me for Thanksgiving, Christmas and Easter dinners. And I got to know their children, who were my age. Knowing the Bernards helped me heal the wound of being excluded or feeling like an orphan.

In April of 1999, I got a call late one night from my father.

"I've got some bad news, Barbara. Susan is dead. The state police found her body at the cabin."

I was shocked and started to ask about the how and when.

"I'll let you know more when I know more. Her body is now at the medical examiner's office. So we have to plan a funeral," he said.

"Dad, call Snowden's. Richard Snowden was a class-mate of Susan's, so let him handle all the arrangements," I said, referring to the funeral home in Wilkes-Barre.

It turned out that Susan had had cirrhosis of the liver, and even though she'd stopped drinking, it was too late. She died, alone in the cabin, of esophageal bleeding. When friends of hers dropped by to visit, they discovered her body and called the police.

Her funeral was on a cold, rainy day in Wilkes-Barre, at the Oak Lawn Cemetery, where the family plot is. I drove from Connecticut, Dad and Dorothy flew up from Key

Biscayne, and Wilkes-Barre friends filled the small Oak Lawn chapel.

Dad asked me to give the eulogy. When I did, I started by saying that no one had the right to criticize Susan for how she lived her life.

"If you weren't there when she was growing up, then you have no idea about what kind of childhood she endured," I said, looking at Dorothy, who was not always kind to Susan.

I spoke at length about Susan's many good and sweet aspects. I wanted people to remember her for those things.

Much to Dorothy's credit, she made amends by finding a home for Susan's four orphaned cats, for which I was very grateful.

On the drive back to Connecticut that day, I was full of remorse about not making the effort to see Susan over the winter. We'd made tentative plans a couple of times, but I always cancelled because I was too lazy to make the three-hour drive.

It had been three and a half years since I'd seen her, at Dad's birthday party in 1995. I vowed I would never again cancel a visit to anyone because of laziness. It was a primary example of carpe diem— seize the day—because you never know when something is the last time.

I mourned Susan's death for a long time. We not only had the same mother; we'd had the same enemy. Peggy's treatment of Susan was brutal, and it started when she was so young.

I remembered the words of the counselor who ran her intervention: "It looks like Susan is going to crash into the basement." I'm convinced she couldn't withstand the child-hood pain without drinking and drugging.

I'd moved up and down the East Coast, from West Redding to Rockport, Massachusetts, to Norfolk, Virginia, to Princeton, New Jersey. Even though I became adept at breaking camp and setting up camp, I was really tired of it.

After my sixty-fourth birthday, I'd had it with uprooting. I wanted to find a place to call home for Act Three. In the fall of 2006, I took a weekend trip to Ojai, California, thirty-five miles south of Santa Barbara. It was a charming little artsy town in the mountains, with a bit of West Coast woo-woo. People looked happier and healthier than people I knew on the East Coast. I had a feeling about the place.

On the flight home, I cried all the way back to Conecticut. That's how much my heart was pulled to Ojai. At the office the next day, I got a call from a friend who asked if I wanted a pet-sitting job for ten weeks.

Oh, hello, universe! This was the way to move to Ojai. I could save a bundle because of no rent or utilities for two months. I met the pet owners, took the job and lived at their rescue-animal farm while they were away training their pets for a Broadway musical and a movie.

I quit my Dow-Jones newspaper job, put all my things in the Bernards' barn and left my dear springer spaniel, Tracy, with them. They loved Tracy, and she had bed privileges there. Meanwhile, I was sixty miles away caring for twelve dogs, four cats, two barn cats, three horses, a Shetland pony, a miniature burro and two llamas. Feeding time required a lot of scheduling.

Before the pet-sitting job began, I drove to Pennsylvania to see my father for his ninety-first birthday. He and

Dorothy were visiting for their annual stopover from Nantucket to Key Biscayne. When I got to the cabin late afternoon, Dad was drunk. He slurred a "hello" from his chair, and his demeanor was fuzzy. Cocktail hour had started.

While he was paying attention to my current springer, Tracy, (he always had a bigger greeting for the dogs than he did for his daughters), I went to the kitchen and brought back a plate of cheese and crackers. That helped sober him up a little. When Dorothy emerged from the bedroom, I suggested that we eat early because I was hungry. So we drove to the nearby roadhouse, and Harrison sobered up some more after having some food. That allowed us to catch up on family news about the summer. Before dinner, I decided not to spend the night. Instead, I said goodbye after the meal and drove home to my cottage on the Hudson River.

The day after, on Monday afternoon, I had my last appointment with Steve. When I told him about the visit and finding my father drunk, he asked how I felt. I told him that I wasn't upset or bothered by it. I felt oddly calm about something that used to drive me nuts.

He looked at me and said, "It seems that you've got no more quarrel with your father and that you've worked them out. You're ready to meet someone without having to deal with unresolved issues with your father. Now you're ready to invite a really nice man into your life."

I took that in and sat quietly for a minute. Then I told him about my plan to move to California, and that I wouldn't be in Manhattan again. This was goodbye. I gave him a hug and felt fortunate to have done so much powerful work with a gifted therapist. I had started seeing Steve in 1993 for a year and then again for the past six months. Steve was instrumental in helping me work through my issues with my father.

When the animal-farm job was over, I house-sat for the Bernards while they were in Florida for a month. That gave me time to organize my things, have my few pieces of furniture and boxes shrink-wrapped on the three pallets for shipping (with an address to come); shipping my files and clothes to a pal's house in Ojai; and packing the car with enough room for Tracy and her dog bed. I stored everything else in Betsy's basement. Anything left over went to the Salvation Army, including the mink coat.

19 *2007–2009*

IT WAS SNOWING and sleeting hard the evening I pulled out of the Bernards' Connecticut driveway. An hour south, it stopped but was still cold and windy. This was a major reason I was leaving New England. I just couldn't stand the cold any more.

I knew I was taking a leap of faith, but I felt prepared. I had money in the bank, had found a place to stay in Santa Barbara, my car was reliable, and I knew my route, thanks to Triple-A Tour Books, which listed dog-friendly motels with high-speed internet, so making reservations along the way was easy. I headed to Asheville, North Carolina, to visit for several days with an old friend from Madrid. Then it was due west on Route 66, now I-40.

The twenty-four-hundred-mile drive from Asheville to Santa Barbara, California, meant driving five hundred miles a day. During the drive I spent most of the time listening to the English historian Simon Schama's eight-disc history of Great Britain. It was heaven.

At night, I set up my computer in my motel room and answered ads on Craigslist for jobs in Santa Barbara. It was easy to send my resume and clips with my cover letter.

It was a Sunday evening when I arrived at the house in Montecito, the very pricey village next to Santa Barbara. I drove up the driveway to a lushly landscaped mansion that turned out to have ten bedrooms, a pool, and tennis courts on two acres.

The woman with whom I was staying lived in Los Angeles during the week, so Tracy and I had the place to ourselves. We were staying in a downstairs suite, a large bedroom and bathroom with a study.

The next day, Monday, I got a call from one of the ads I'd answered, and set up an interview for Tuesday. The interview went well and the magazine editor offered me a job, starting right away. So I began work Wednesday as a writer for a trade magazine.

All the stars were in alignment. I'd found a very nice place to live and an equally nice place to work, all in the same week.

I didn't want to leave Tracy alone in a strange house, so I took her to work with me. She stayed in the car and slept (she was 12 and slept a lot, no matter where she was). On my breaks, I took her for walks, and after work, we walked on the beach where she chased seagulls. We were both happy being outside in the warm sunshine in March.

The second week at the magazine, my editor mentioned that he lived in Ojai and that he and his wife were moving from their one-bedroom cottage.

"So what's the name and number of your old landlord?" I asked.

I called right away, and made a date to meet her the next day. After seeing the cottage and having a walk-through, I gave her a check and references for myself and Tracy. The place was adorable, complete with French doors and a white picket fence. I had Tracy with me, and the landlady liked her. Having a dog was no problem. The landlady sent me a lease, and I moved in three weeks later.

By the time my furniture arrived, I'd made a deal with the magazine to work from home and drive to Santa Barbara once a week to meet with my editor. Perfect, no commuting.

Finally, I had all my things under one roof. It had been a six-month transition and three moves from my first visit to Ojai to moving into this sweet little cottage. I was tired and decided to dedicate the summer for rest and restoration.

I bought a three-speed English bike to pedal around Ojai, joined the Athletic Club so I could swim every day, take a yoga class and walk Tracy twice a day for the mile-long loop around town. After years of working nights and all the moving, I was exhausted. It was time to get fit as well as happy.

The home and the job had come to fruition. Now all I had to do was wait for the nice man to make himself known. I remembered Cynde's advice: "Let it happen, DeWitt. You don't have to make it happen. Trust the universe."

Three months later, I met a man at a gathering of some new friends. At the end of the evening, he asked if I'd like to join him for coffee. It was fun having a coffee date, my first date in a very long time. We talked and laughed easily and discovered we had a lot of mutual interests. He was from Los Angeles and was visiting Ojai for the weekend. After coffee, we walked Tracy, and he asked what I was looking for.

"Well, I've never been a sucker for a pretty face," I said.

"So you're looking for a fat, bald man?"

"No," I laughed. "I'm looking for a nice man."

He took my hand and gave it a gentle squeeze, and we walked in silence until we got back to my cottage. He asked if I'd like to have dinner with him the next night.

"I'd love to."

And that's how I came to have a gentleman caller. Dinner the next night was lovely. After that, Fred drove to Ojai every weekend, bringing me flowers and courting me.

Later that fall, the magazine job came to an end because of the economic crash of 2007. I found a job at the daily Santa Barbara News-Press, and once again, synchronicity played a part. The editor who interviewed me discovered we had worked at the same paper in Virginia, just not at the same time. When I told him who my best friend was at the paper, he said, "Mine, too."

He picked up his phone and called our mutual friend.

"Hey, Wayne, guess who I'm interviewing? DeWitt. She's right here, right now. OK. Yeah. Yeah. OK. Thanks, pal. I'll be in touch."

"Wayne says you're cool. Can you start working tonight?"

Well, that was a pretty fast vetting. I needed a day to put my affairs in order and started work two days later. A year and a half later, I was let go, along with some other editors whose jobs were also cut. A thirty-year career in the newspaper business had come to an end.

By then, Tracy had died. I decided to move to Los Angeles, to be near Fred, who has turned out to be the love of my life.

That summer, Fred and I went to Nantucket for my father's 94th birthday. We flew to Boston and drove to Betsy's house in western Massachusetts so I could get all the boxes I had stored there. The boxes contained my Tiffany crystal glasses; my grandmother's Limoges—dinner plates, two sets of dessert plates and salad plates, all different patterns she got when she was in France in 1906 during her Grand Tour with her parents; a mahogany box containing a sterling silver setting for twelve, plus serving utensils, fish knives with mother-of-pearl handles and demi-tasse spoons; a slew of good dishes from Crate and Barrel and kitchen things from Pottery Barn. The plan was to take everything to UPS for packing and shipping to California and then drive back to Hyannis to get the Nantucket ferry.

Fred and I got to Betsy's about nine at night, and introduced ourselves to her housemate, who was expecting us. In the morning, Fred and I went down to the basement. It took me about 15 seconds to see that the space where I had stacked the dozen or so boxes on pallets was empty. The pallets were there, but nothing else. I blinked, took another hard look and did a quick survey of all the other boxes in her basement. None of them were mine.

"Oh, no, Fred, everything's gone. Nothing's here," I gasped.

"Oh, sweetheart, no," he said and held me close to him.

In that moment, right there, I had an epiphany: "I'd rather have love than Limoges."

I'd grown up with beautiful things, had been married and lived in homes with beautiful things, been divorced and had my own things. And all the time I was moving from house to house, with all my beautiful things, I felt lonely and unloved. Now I felt loved and wouldn't trade that for anything.

"What do you want to do, sweetheart?" Fred asked after the long silence.

"Let's head to Hyannis and get the ferry."

We put our bags in the car and headed east. During the three-hour drive, I told Fred about how Betsy had rented a room to a guy who had been delinquent in paying his rent, and who ended up stealing some of her things. That happened the previous summer when she was on Nantucket. She didn't discover the missing things until fall. Now I knew who had stolen my things: the thief who'd been living in her house.

Betsy met us at the ferry, and we drove out to 'Sconset to the cottage she'd gotten for us. And we settled in for the weekend.

The next night was meet-the-family night. We had dinner at the Sankaty Golf Club, and Fred met Dad and Dorothy, and Marjorie and Betsy and their respective boyfriends. I sat next to Dorothy and got caught up after a four-year absence. The meal was delicious, nobody was drinking excessively and all during dinner friends dropped by the table to greet Harrison, wish him "Happy Birthday" and say hello to me.

The next morning I went over to Betsy's place.

"Hi, Ba. Well, that Fred is a charmer," she said.

"I know, I know. What's not to love?" I asked.

"No wonder you're radiant. I've never seen you look so happy," she said.

"It's true, Betsy. I've never been happier," I said.

On the flight back to California, Fred said he would like us to live together. "But I just don't know how to work that out yet."

A week later, Fred called.

"Can you get over here? We've got a house to see," he said.

Fred had a neighbor three houses away from his little bachelor cottage, where he'd lived for nine years after his divorce. Over the past year, the neighbor Judy and I had become friendly during my visits to Fred. She had just finished renovating her big house and had moved into the studio behind it. Now she was ready to rent it.

"I didn't want smokers, or kids or loud music, and I didn't want the hassle of having to sort through a lot of applications. I think this house suits you and Fred," she said.

It was a beautiful old house with wood floors, two bedrooms, two bathrooms, a big laundry room and pantry, and an L-shaped enclosed veranda in front. While Judy gave us a tour, I smiled at Fred and nodded yes. He did the same and squeezed my hand.

"Well, what do you think?" Judy asked.

"I think it's gorgeous. I'd love to live here," I answered.

"When do you want to move it, December or January?"

"How about December?" I said. "Then we can be here for Fred's birthday and for Christmas."

"December would be good," Fred said in his quiet, collected way.

Judy mentioned a price; we shook hands and had a deal.

On the way back to his cottage, we couldn't believe our good fortune—a spacious, beautiful home that was affordable for us.

Two months later, we moved in, in time for his birthday, a housewarming party and Christmas with his father.

A year later, we got a dog. Finally, I had a dog again in a home of my own with a man I love and who loves me. I hit the lotto!

My life had stabilized, and the unfinished business seemed done.

20 *2012*

THE PHONE RANG at 8 o'clock Sunday morning, New Year's Day. I was having a cup of tea and reading my New York Times.

"Happy New Year," I answered.

"Barbara, it's Henninger. I'm so sorry about the news."

It was a cousin in New York, and I had no idea what he was talking about.

"Hi, Henninger. What news?"

"Oh, didn't anyone call you?" He hesitated, then said: "Your father died earlier today, just after midnight. I'm sorry no one called you about it."

Dad was dead?

I wasn't really shocked by Dad's death. After all, he was 96 years old, had led a full, active life, and his mind was still very much in tact. He and Dorothy regularly played bridge and Scrabble on Key Biscayne and Nantucket. And he was a daily newspaper reader, a habit of a lifetime, as well as an avid reader, primarily histories and biographies. He loved reading the Edmund Morris trilogy on Theodore Roosevelt, whose grandson was a Nantucket friend.

After speaking with Dorothy to learn the details, I told her I'd write the obituaries to send to the three newspapers where he had lived: Miami, Wilkes-Barre and Nantucket. The task gave me time to reflect on Dad's childhood, his schooling, war service, three marriages and five daughters. He had the good fortune to die gracefully, a cardiac arrest at home, just after New Year's Eve, with no lingering or suffering. No fuss. No muss. Lights out, period. Just the way he liked it. I should be so lucky to die that way.

Several days later, Dorothy called and announced that she'd had Dad cremated. What? I was shocked because in my last conversation with him, he was adamant about *not* being cremated. "Noooo, I don't want to be cremated," he said in an agitated voice. "I want to be buried in Wilkes-Barre, in our family plot where my mother and father are buried, and where my sister and the rest of the family are."

Unfortunately, he forgot to tell Dorothy, and it never occurred to her ask me or my sisters about what he wanted.

But as Dorothy explained it, she ran into a neighbor, a recent widow, who told her: "I have two words for you—Neptune Society."

She gave Dorothy a brochure, Dorothy made a call, and the Neptune Society, the cremation organization, picked up my father's body from the Miami-Dade County Medical Examiner's office a few days later. And that was that.

In an instant I knew what had happened. Dorothy had been too overwhelmed to deal with all the arrangements and logistics about flying a body from one state to another, especially in the winter, when cemetery grounds are frozen and no digging can be done until the spring, when the weather warms up.

Moreover, Dorothy didn't know who or what to call in Wilkes-Barre. One phone call to the Neptune Society solved all those problems.

I understood and so didn't mention his insistence on not being cremated. The deed was done, and there was no point in flogging a dead horse, so to speak.

"Of course, I understand, Dorothy. Just do what's easiest

for you," I told her. "But we need to pick a date for the Key Biscayne memorial because four of us have to make plane reservations to get there." I suggested an upcoming long weekend, and she agreed.

Two weeks later Marjorie and I flew to Miami from California, and Rosanne and her companion, Laura, drove from Georgia. Betsy wasn't coming from western Massachusetts. She said she planned to be at the two other memorials, one in Nantucket during the summer and the final one in Wilkes-Barre in the fall.

On Saturday morning, we all met inside the Key Biscayne Presbyterian Church where the service was being held. The widow and my sisters and I were dressed in black, in contrast to the colorful garb worn by so many of the other women.

When I saw Dorothy, I gave her a big hug. She looked dazed and seemed glad when I said I'd take charge of the family seating. I pointed to where she and I were going to sit (as widow and the oldest child, in the front pew), and put our handbags there to reserve our places.

Some of her seven grandchildren were already seated there, and I directed them across the aisle, to sit behind their parents.

When the church was full and Dorothy sat down, an older man in a Veterans khaki uniform appeared at her side and asked if he could give a brief eulogy at the end. Dad had been a member of the Key Biscayne Veterans of Foreign War, which met at the yacht club to play bridge and enjoy cocktails. Dorothy looked at me, and I nodded yes to Dr. Mags, a Key Biscayne surgeon and Vietnam veteran.

The minister began the service by mentioning his own connection to Wilkes-Barre. When he finished, Rosanne and I gave our eulogies, followed with musical recitals by Dorothy's children and grandchildren.

At the end, Dr. Mags walked to the podium and spoke of his friendship with Dad, and talked about how Harrison Smith had been a real patriot as a soldier in the Pacific Theater of War during the Second World War. He then told two humorous stories about Dad's bridge playing, and when he finished, the good doctor announced he was going to play Taps.

With that, he walked to the back of the church, onto the steps beyond the open door, raised the bugle to his lips and played Taps. I turned around to watch and after the last note, I saw him drop onto the church steps.

I looked around at the congregation, who were leaving their pews to go to the opposite side to the reception area. None of them had seen Dr. Mags collapse.

I rushed to the back of the church just in time to see the Key Biscayne ambulance and EMS personnel drive up to where Dr. Mags was lying. One of the VFW men had called 911, and the ambulance and EMS guys were there in less than a minute. An EMS responder checked his pulse, shook his head and walked to the ambulance, came back with a stretcher, put a sheet over him, and the men carried the body back to the ambulance. It turns out the ambulance was parked right next door, at the firehouse, which explains how it got there so fast.

What irony. Dr. Mags had played Taps for Dad as well as for himself. The last note turned out to be *his* last note. The doctor had had a cardiac arrest and dropped dead on the church steps.

When I went back inside the church and told someone about what I had seen, he said, "What do you mean Dr. Mags just dropped dead? You're joking, right?"

The day after the service, I paid a visit to Dorothy. I

hadn't been to the Key Biscayne condo in twenty-one years, not since I'd left Miami.

For three hours, I mostly listened. To be fair, her husband of twenty-two years had just died, and Dorothy's need to talk was greater than usual. I asked a question about her childhood and heard a very sad story, an orphan's tale. It explained so much, why she was not attuned to so many things. Her mother died when she was a baby, and because her father was a traveling salesman, she'd been deposited in the care of different and indifferent relatives. As a result, she had no parental guidance or financial security. No one had educated her about the finer points of life; for her, it was all about survival. It was the Depression and she said, "We were poor, very poor."

While Dorothy was telling her story, I didn't interrupt for any clarifications; I just listened. Her older brother managed to get himself to college in Michigan, and when their father died, he sent for her. The two of them found a place to live while he finished his medical studies. He was 20, she was 12, and it was light years away from Mississippi and all her known reference points. She'd been another unguided orphan just trying to make sense of her upside-down world, and I felt a lot of compassion for this woman whose life had been turned upside down, once again, by death.

My father had been the focus and point of her life, and she had taken very good care of him. Now she had lost that focus, and everything seemed pointless to her, she said.

"I thought of ending my own life, Barbara. That way, I could be with Harrison."

"Dorothy, that's a normal thought for anyone who's just lost a spouse. But you can't do anything like that because of your children and grandchildren. You know that, don't you?" I said softly. And I reached my hand across the coffee table to hold her hand.

"Yes, I know," she murmured.

When she got up to use the bathroom, I stood and stretched and looked around. Dorothy had redone the living room. At least the old bookcase was there, and I walked over to look at some family photographs. I was familiar with most of them, but one stopped me in my tracks. It was a picture of my father, my mother and me when I was a baby. I'd never seen it. I didn't have any photos of my mother and me because Peggy had destroyed them all during one of her drunken rages.

Seeing this photo of the three of us smiling and happy stunned me. My father held a little stuffed toy and stood behind my mother, who was seated and holding me in her lap. It was the Smith family Christmas card from 1942, with my grandparents and my father's sister and brother. The Smith joie de vivre and Christmas cheer were evident, even in a photo.

The picture showed a sweet-looking baby with doting parents and grandparents. The picture showed that I was loved, and it was like having a missing piece of a puzzle drift back into place, 70 years later.

When Dorothy returned to the living room, I told her that I'd never seen that photo and how touched I was by it.

Five minutes later, I said goodbye. Before I left, I took a look around, knowing this was the last time I'd see the place. My father had owned the apartment for 15 years before he married Dorothy, and I'd lived there for a year and a half when I first moved to Miami, when he was still the merry widower.

The following week, I received a FedEx envelope from Dorothy. There was a copy of the family photo of my mother and father and me. It was a priceless memento and I was deeply touched by her gesture.

21 *Summer 2012*

THAT SUMMER, DOROTHY sent two other packages with photographs and documents: my parents' marriage license, their divorce papers, and photo albums of me as an infant and toddler. This trove also included my father's Army records.

When I was examining the dates—from when he was sent to training and then to Tokyo and Korea for the post-war U.S. occupation—I noticed the dates of his discharge. He was overseas nine months before Susan was born. Oh, my god. He couldn't have fathered Susan. I counted back nine months on my fingertips from her birth. Oh, hell, that meant Peggy had been right. Susan *was* Ross Payson's child. She was blond and blue-eyed, just like his other three children with Mother, a fact I had always tried to ignore.

While I was sitting at my desk in Los Angeles, trying to reconcile this new information, a torrent of memories flooded me.

The first flashback was from twenty-nine years ago, a night when Susan and I were sitting with Dad on the balcony of the Key Biscayne condo. Susan was visiting from Connecticut and was chatting about this and that. Suddenly, she got quiet and said: "Dad, I'm so glad you're my father."

I shot a quick look at my father who became uncharacteristically misty-eyed. He cleared his throat and said in a quiet voice, "Me, too, Susan," and reached for her hand on the table and squeezed it.

The following night, after Susan had flown home, Dad and I were on the balcony having cocktails, and he said: "I know how rough it was for you, Barbara. She told me that she loved children, and I needed a wife and a mother for you girls." His oblique explanation was as specific as he was willing to get, about how he came to marry Peggy, although he never mentioned her name.

The second memory was a conversation with my half-brother, Rick, who lives outside of Philadelphia. I'd called him because I wanted to visit my mother's grave, to put flowers on it. I'd been there once, for her funeral, but didn't know the name of the cemetery, let alone where her grave was. I asked if he would drive me there. At the time, I was living in Princeton, New Jersey, an hour away.

On the drive to the cemetery, Rick told me a story his father had told him. Apparently when Dad was overseas and on a day when Marjorie and I were in school, Ross and Mother were having an afternoon tryst. But my grandmother called, and when my mother tried to put her off from visiting by saying she was sick, Granny became concerned. She told my mother that she'd be right over with some soup.

My grandmother lived just five minutes away, so Ross had no time to make a get-away, and he hid underneath the bed while Granny visited. Rick was laughing the whole time he told the story. I didn't see anything funny because it was a story of betrayal to my father. But it confirmed for me when Mother and Ross had started their affair.

During that same trip to my mother's gravesite, I stayed with an old family friend from Wilkes-Barre, a woman who had been my nursery-school teacher. That night I asked Aunt Bonnie what she knew about Ross and mother.

"Well, you were about three and very chatty, like three-year-olds are. A couple of times when you arrived at nursery school in the morning, you blurted out, 'Uncle Ross spent the weekend with us.' The other teacher and I looked at each other and nodded. So we knew what was going on," she said.

All of this new information led me to the obvious and unanswered question: Why the hell would Ross and mother give up their first-born? And how did it all come about?

The next memory I had was from forty-three years ago, the last night I lived with my mother.

"I *never* would have agreed to the terms of the divorce if I had known that Peggy would come into your life and treat you girls the way she did," she said and started to cry. "But your father could give you girls everything—private schools, a beautiful home, all the nice things I could never have given you."

When I saw her sobbing, I realized for the first time what a terrible loss and hardship she must have gone through not having custody of her three daughters. From what she said, I gathered that the custody decision hadn't been hers. The phrase, "agreed to the terms," indicated that someone else had presented her with a plan for a divorce agreement. The only person who could have done that was my grandmother. She was, after all, the family matriarch upon her husband's death in December 1945.

Working backwards from June 7, 1946, Susan's birth, I guessed my mother must have told Granny about the pregnancy sometime in January 1946, when she was four months along.

Even though the war was over by January 1946, my

father's discharge didn't take effect until April. So Granny had to come up with a plan to salvage the honor of her first-born.

My father was Granny's first born and favorite child. As he was going to inherit the title of publisher of the Wilkes-Barre Publishing Company, I know she wanted to protect his position and reputation. The matriarch was not going to let Prince Hal be a cuckold, to be publicly shamed by his wife giving birth to another man's child.

The punishment for my mother's transgression was my father getting custody of the children. Furthermore, the new child would have the Smith name and, after a no-fuss Reno divorce (six weeks residency in Nevada for an uncontested divorce), Mother would be exiled.

Susan was born in June 1946, the Reno divorce was in September, Ross and mother were married promptly and moved to Chicago, not only out of town, but out of state.

It was all so neat and tidy, just like my grandmother. She ran a very tight ship. The divorce agreement gave Mother custody of Susan until a certain age, and then my father got custody.

The memories just kept coming, eager to reveal themselves. The next one was Aunt Lois's drunken confession to me about how Peggy showed up in the spring of 1947. Peggy would have been twenty-nine, unmarried and living with her mother in a Philadelphia suburban apartment. In those days, that made her an old maid. But as I was told by one of Peggy's friends, as soon as she heard about my father's divorce, Peggy called Aunt Lois, who had been a former schoolmate, and invited herself to Wilkes-Barre. During her visit, she manipulated Aunt Lois to invite Dad over for cocktails. Three and a half months later, Peggy and Dad were married. She moved like a shark going in for the kill. Aunt Lois said that she never heard from Peggy after the wedding.

Later that week, in Los Angeles, I made an appointment with a therapist to help me with an issue that I wanted to resolve. I was mentoring a personality-disordered woman and wanted to distance myself from her gracefully because I couldn't deal with her crazy behavior any more. The therapist knew of this woman and knew she was a borderline personality disorder.

The day of the appointment, I talked about the issue without spending time doing a family history. She already knew a great deal about my background. I explained that I needed help in moving this woman out of my life and mentioned that I'd previously mentored another borderline personality disorder.

"Who was the borderline personality in your household?" she asked point blank.

The question hit me like a slap in the face.

"Oh, my God, Peggy was the borderline. She was my stepmother. That explains why she was so crazy," I blurted out.

I knew from all the research I'd done what the borderline characteristics are—someone incapable of impulse control or adult reasoning; someone addicted to chaos and drama, who lacks executive functioning ability, who deflects confrontation by raging and is given to lability—fast-moving mood swings. Further description includes irrational and extreme jealousy, inappropriate behavior, and denial of inappropriate or childish behavior.

This explained why Peggy never made a list, couldn't balance a checkbook, why her room and bathroom were always such a mess, or that she would never, ever apologize for her bad behavior and tantrums. On top of that, there was her alcoholism and daily use of prescription pills, the bowl of tranquilizers that she kept on her bedside table like a candy bowl filled with M&Ms. No wonder she spent so much time in bed. She was sleeping off the hangovers or in a stupor with the tranquilizers. She was taking phenobarbital by the handful.

Now everything about her made sense.

When I got home later, I called Peggy's nephew to share my new information. His mother was Peggy's older sister.

"It all makes sense," he said.

Growing up, we all knew she was crazy, but now I knew why. There was a diagnosis that just hadn't been made.

No wonder Dad went outside the marriage to find comfort and companionship. The first woman I heard about was someone he'd met at the Pennsylvania Institute when he was hospitalized for three months. For years, he'd had rendezvous with her. I found this out through Susan, who was living in Philadelphia, and she saw them several times at the same restaurant. Somebody else must have spotted them, too, because I remember hearing one of the inebriated grownups in Wilkes-Barre say, "You know, Hal fell in love with a woman he met in Philadelphia."

That explained all those trips he took to Philadelphia under the guise of newspaper business.

22 *Fall 2012–Spring 2013*

THE OCTOBER TRIP to Wilkes-Barre for the funeral was another illuminating journey. Marjorie and I each booked our own rooms for privacy. Betsy and Rosanne stayed with a friend, while Dorothy and her son, as well as her nephew, niece and niece's spouse were bunked in the cabin, thirty miles away.

After the funeral, Dorothy hosted a luncheon at the Westmoreland Club in a private room for all the family members who had traveled from out of town. Last summer I got the idea that my sisters and I host a dinner party for our school friends. All our friends had known Dad from the Day School and dancing class and parties at Shrine View. They also loved him and his colorful antics.

The dinner party the Smith sisters threw at the Westmoreland Club was wonderful. The four of us hadn't seen each other since the memorial service in January on Key Biscayne, when we were in the first stage of grief about Dad's death. Tonight was a happy night, a chance to see people we'd known since childhood. During dinner, we all raised a glass in memory of Harrison and shared lots of funny stories about him.

The next day was the funeral. After the minister concluded the service, a VFW group that Dorothy contacted showed up to play Taps. But the bugler was not really playing the bugle. Instead, it was a recording, a tinny little sound coming from the bugle. And after the VFW man presented a folded flag to Dorothy, the funereal mood was broken when, at her insistence, the cemetery's small Bobcat started to move the dirt piled by the side of the hole for the urn and grind noisily, back and forth and back and forth, until Dad's urn was covered, just five feet from where everyone was still seated.

Well, at least the pretend trumpeter didn't drop dead at the funeral like the Key Biscayne service.

The following spring, I got a call from Dorothy who said she wanted to empty the Miami storage unit with the last of Dad's boxes. Rosanne had taken the first batch after the memorial service in January. This time, I wanted to be the curator for all the remaining things, to make sure the photos were safely stored in acid-free photo albums. I called my cousin Jim to ask if I could stay with him in South Florida.

On the appointed day, Dorothy and I met at the storage unit, where there were about forty boxes—one long row of cartons, stacked four high. I brought a box-cutter and some rubber gloves to protect my hands, some tunafish sandwiches and lots of bottled water on ice in a small Igloo. Dorothy brought two folding chairs for us while we worked in the unit. Even with the shade, the metal storage unit was like an oven with the eighty-five degree heat. The boxes were all caked with dirt and grime and breaking apart at the seams. They'd been in storage for thirty-two years, from when Dad sold Shrine View and moved to Florida.

I brought out my box-cutter and started working my way though the forty boxes, slitting them open and determining whether they went to the dump or to the trunk of my rented car. I had to work fast because the storage place closed at 3 p.m. on Sundays. Every once in a while, I stopped to linger over some photos—ones of my grandmother, or my cousins and aunts and uncles. Every time I saw a photo of my mother and me, I took a deep breath. And every photo I saw of Peggy and her beady eyes went into the trash bag.

Dorothy kept chatting about this and that, but one remark made me stop.

"Your father mourned terribly about Peggy," she chattered.

I was not going to let this lie fly.

"Dorothy, let me set the record straight. Three weeks after Peggy died, my father had his Florida girlfriend at Shrine View and the cabin, where she stayed for a week. And as soon as they returned to Florida, they went out in public, and everybody knew they were a couple."

She looked at me quietly, and then spoke: "But Arlene ran off with another man."

"Dorothy, that was four years later. Arlene told me she broke it off with Dad after years of putting up with his drinking. She told me his drunken behavior was just awful and she couldn't take it any more. So she left for Chicago, where she had met a man from her office. He wasn't a drunk, which is why she married him," I told her.

She gave me a "deer-in-the-headlight" expression. "I didn't know you spoke with Arlene."

"Of course I spoke with Arlene. We all did because she was included in family gatherings and dinners. That's why she made a point of calling me about her decision to leave. Arlene was a very nice woman," I said.

Dorothy was silent, and I thought that was enough truth for the day, and went back to plowing through the boxes.

When I was done, twenty-five boxes were designated

for the dump, and I took fifteen boxes back to Jim's. When I got to his house, I emptied the boxes and put the contents onto a drop cloth and sorted through everything. The next day I repacked all the photos and papers into new boxes, which Jim taped up and labeled. I sent a box of my grandfather's war memorabilia to my cousin Ernie, my grandfather's namesake. I shipped the other thirteen boxes home to Los Angeles.

The next day, I said goodbye to Jim and flew north. It was springtime in New York, and the tulips and daffodils were everywhere, flowers that are not native to Los Angeles. I loved seeing the steady stream of spring colors up and down Park Avenue and flowing from window boxes hanging from brownstones. I also felt so energized walking everywhere, and getting some cultural and cerebral nourishment from friends, like the writer I was staying with. Even the French hairdresser is an intellectual. But of course; he's French.

I also had an appointment with Steve Kirschner, the Jungian therapist, the one who told me "When you've found a nice loving man, you will have broken with your family history."

I walked into Steve's office and sat down in the old familiar chair. I told him about the trip to Miami and about all the secrets about Susan and the engineered divorce that I'd pieced together that winter.

Then I shared my recent revelation about my role in the family. I'd been the Keeper of Secrets. All my years of listening and watching and having drunken adults confide in me meant that I carried the institutional memory of the family. Now that Zeus was dead, I was free to write the history, secrets and all. My role as Keeper of the Secrets had also died.

When I told Steve about a lingering reluctance to break my silence, he said, "Everybody's dead. It doesn't matter."

Ah, right. The lingering reluctance was tied to an old ACOA dynamic: the no-talk rule. Now I was liberated from that. I gave Steve a parting hug and thanked him for all his help.

Once the Florida boxes arrived in Los Angeles, sorting through them was simple. I made obvious piles: photos in one; letters in another; newspapers in another. There were newspapers a century old, including the account of my grandparents' wedding; newspapers with reports from the warfront of the First World War, written by my grandfather, who described trench fighting and "warding off the Hun." Reading his war dispatches was like reading Hemingway.

Going through the photos took two days, and I sorted them by generations. One photo included four generations: my father as an infant, seated in the lap of his great-grandmother, Jennie Dowling DeWitt, with his grandmother, Jennie DeWitt Harvey, and his mother, Marjorie Harvey Smith, standing to each side. The photo was taken in 1916, when Dad was only six months old, Granny was thirty, her mother fifty-seven, her grandmother was eighty-seven. It was reassuring to see that I came from a line of women who had kind faces.

Near the end of the sorting, I came across a photo that caused me to gasp. It was of my mother, taken when she was twenty-one, done in a 1940s portrait style—a black and white head-and-shoulders shot, a three-quarters profile. Mother looked so lovely.

That afternoon I bought a pretty frame, and when I got home and put the picture on my mantel, I realized this was the first time I'd ever had a photo of my mother on display. I was so grateful that it had been safely put away in Dad's office files, safe from one of Peggy's drunken rages. The next day was Mother's Day, and I put a rose in a crystal bud vase next to her photo. I'd never been able to honor my mother on Mother's Day.

How ironic that it took the death of my father to resurrect my mother. Putting her photograph on the mantel was closing the book on a long, unfinished story.

23 *Fall 2016*

THERE WERE SEVERAL factors that prompted me to leave Los Angeles: I could no longer stand the noise, the traffic, the summer heat or the general rudeness. Also, I could no longer afford the rent.

So I moved to Palm Springs, two hours south, only to discover very soon after that I'm not a desert person. The searing, relentless summer heat was unbearable, and so were all that brown and beige landscape, including the houses and buildings. But it was kismet. I joined the Palm Springs Writers Guild, and then a month later, found my publisher through an event the Guild was hosting. So I was meant to be there.

Late one night when I was working at my desk, I heard a huge roar, as if a jet were taking off outside my front door. A second later, the floor of the house started rolling, and I grabbed the edges of my desk and hung on to keep my chair from rolling away.

"Oh, Christ, an earthquake. I don't want to die in the

desert. I want to die where I was born," I heard myself say out loud.

The 5.3 earthquake had literally jolted the truth out of me. When the trembler stopped about 30 seconds later, I checked the U.S. Geological Survey website and saw that the epicenter was only three miles away from Palm Springs. As a result, I didn't sleep that night. I was too nervous about any aftershocks.

But while I lay in bed, I started to picture all the mountain greenery and rain and streams and flowers, and the desire to return to Pennsylvania had taken hold. Since my lease in the desert was going to be up in a few months, I made one phone call the next morning, to my dear friend, Jane Graham Kishbaugh, and asked that if she heard of any places for rent to keep me in mind.

"Oh, I'm thinking of renting the apartment at the back of the house where Mother lived. Would that interest you?"

Yes! A sign! And just like that, effortlessly, I found a place to live, in a house where I had spent time as a little girl as well as an adult. It's where I visited with Mrs. Graham before she died and where I stayed when I went back to Wilkes-Barre for a Day School reunion.

After living in Florida for ten years, I moved to Nantucket Island. But my "forever" home washed out to sea, so I left to continue my odyssey in New York City, Princeton, Connecticut and Massachusetts to find a home. Finally, I left the Northeast to find a home where there was no snow and ended up in Southern California in hopes of finding a good job and a good man, and a home, of course.

The drive from Connecticut to California gave me time to look at large chunks of my life. I realized that I was much more ambitious than I had ever admitted. That's why I'd been willing to move so often—to move up the professional ladder of the newspaper world. I'd started late (I was 37 when I got my first newspaper job) and felt I had to make up for lost time. So I forfeited relationships for my career. And I didn't live long enough in any one place to cultivate a relationship.

In California, I found the man, and after seven years in Los Angeles, the relationship had run its course. Circumstances helped push us apart: we lost our lease, we lost the dog and I lost heart. The landlady wanted to move back into her lovely house, and when our sweet Wheaten terrier Charlie died, all the oxygen went out of the relationship for me, although it had started to wither before then.

I will always consider Fred to be my sweetheart and the love of my life. He was the first long relationship I ever had, someone with whom I shared so many wonderful experiences—cultural, social, culinary, traveling, intellectual. But in the long run, he was tae kwon do, and I was tai chi. I had to leave, and so Fred and I parted as respectful, loving friends.

I remember a passage from "Gone With The Wind," and what Rhett Butler said when he explained why he was leaving Atlanta and returning to Charleston: "I want a life lived by gentle folks. I've grown tired of shoddy manners and cheap emotions."

After years in sunny climes among swans who flock to warm places, I want to be among genteel people who know of good manners, practice kind gestures and have a generosity of spirit. I want to live among people I've known for a lifetime and who know me. When I returned to Wyoming Valley and the Back Mountain, it was the first time I'd moved where I was not a stranger. I didn't have to cultivate anything from scratch. I knew the lay of the land.

For a long time, I did not want to be buried in the

family plot. But that has changed, and now I want to have my headstone among the other Smiths. I want to claim my place in the family.

Dad, of course, has two headstones. When Peggy died, he had his name put on a shared tombstone, date of death to be filled in. He hadn't counted on remarrying. So when he died, Dorothy had a new one made with their two names. It's like, "Where's Waldo?" Which grave is Harrison actually buried in? I'm sure Zeus is having a good laugh over this bafflement at the on-going cocktail party in the sky.

I've settled into my new place, feathered my nest and got a dog! He's a sweet old goofy Wheaten-poodle mix named Toby. It's great to wake up again with the dog. God, I love the smell of dog in the morning!

On my seventy-fifth birthday, Betsy drove to Wilkes-Barre from Northampton for dinner at the Westmoreland Club. Sister Marjorie was treating us because she's a member. And as I sat down, Rosanne appeared! She'd flown in from Georgia to surprise me. What a wonderful gift, and I love her for that. The three Smith sisters, all wearing our pearls, couldn't stop laughing, thanks to our healed hearts. It was great to share a loving, wonderful weekend with my sisters.

So I've had my odyssey, seen and done and found many things, including myself. Feeling fulfilled and wise, and armed with endless curiosity, *now* I am home at last.

Books that were essential to my healing and growth

Perfect Daughters	Robert Ackerman
The Ugly Duckling	Hans Christian Andersen
Healing The Shame That Binds You	John Bradshaw
Gods in Every Man	Jean Shinoda Bolen
Goddesses in Every Woman	Jean Shinoda Bolen
The Art of Happiness	Dalai Lama
Identity And The Life Cycle	Erik Erikson
Man's Search for Meaning	Victor Frankl
The Art of Loving	Erich Fromm
Emotional Intelligence	Daniel Goleman
A Primer of Jungian Psychology	Calvin Hall
Learning to Love Yourself	Gay Hendricks
The Portable Jung	Carl Jung
Please Understand Me II	David Keirsey
Callings: Finding an Authentic Life	Gregg LeVoy
I Will Not Die an Unlived Life	Dawn Markof

Care of the Soul	Thomas Moore
Soul Mates	Thomas Moore
Introduction to Type	Isabel Briggs Myers
Anatomy of the Spirit	Carolyn Myss
Women Who Love Too Much	Robin Norwood
The Road Less Traveled	Scott Peck
When Food Is Love	Geneen Roth
Oh The Places You'll Go	Dr. Seuss
A Fine Romance	Judith Sills
Choicemaking	Sharon Wegscheider
Understanding Co-dependency	Sharon Wegscheider Cruse
Journey of the Heart	John Welwood
Adult Children of Alcoholics*	Janet Woititz
Fear of Intimacy	Janet Woititz

* I suggest starting with this book.

Things I learned in therapy

1. 'No' is a complete sentence.

2. I had to deconstruct before I could rebuild my life.

3. Learning not to internalize feedback as criticism.

4. Taking care of myself.

5. How to shut down the constant internal stream of criticism.

6. Being detached about what others think of me.

7. Making sense of my childhood and not repeating the past.

8. Letting go of the fantasy that someone will rescue me.

9. Asking for help is a sign of good mental health.

10. Life has two columns: Blessings and Blessings in Disguise.

DeWitt Smith had a 30-year career as a newspaper, magazine and online journalist, as an editor and features writer. She now works as a freelance book editor. This is her first book.

.

CPSIA information can be obtained
at www.ICGtesting.com
Printed in the USA
BVOW11s1414220517

484736BV00001B/2/P

9 781627 874533